THE ART OF THE LOOM

D0521449

San Diego Christian College
2100 Greenfield Drive
El Cajon, CA 92019

746.14
H447a

26.96

THE ART OF THE LOOM

Weaving, spinning and dyeing across the world

Ann Hecht

University of Washington Press
Seattle

For Hermann

Frontispiece
Peruvian woman sitting in a doorway
weaving on the simplest of looms.
The warp threads are held under tension
between her waist and her foot.
By her side lies a pile of warp-patterned
belts for sale.

© 1989, 2001 Ann Hecht
Published by The British Museum Press
A division of The British Museum Company Ltd
46 Bloomsbury Street, London WC1B 3QQ

First published 1989
First published in paperback 2001

Published in the United States of America by the
University of Washington Press, PO Box 50096,
Seattle, WA 98145-5096.

ISBN 0-295-98139-3

Designed by Trevor and Jacqui Vincent
Phototypeset by Southern Positives and Negatives (SPAN),
Lingfield, Surrey
Printed in Hong Kong

CONTENTS

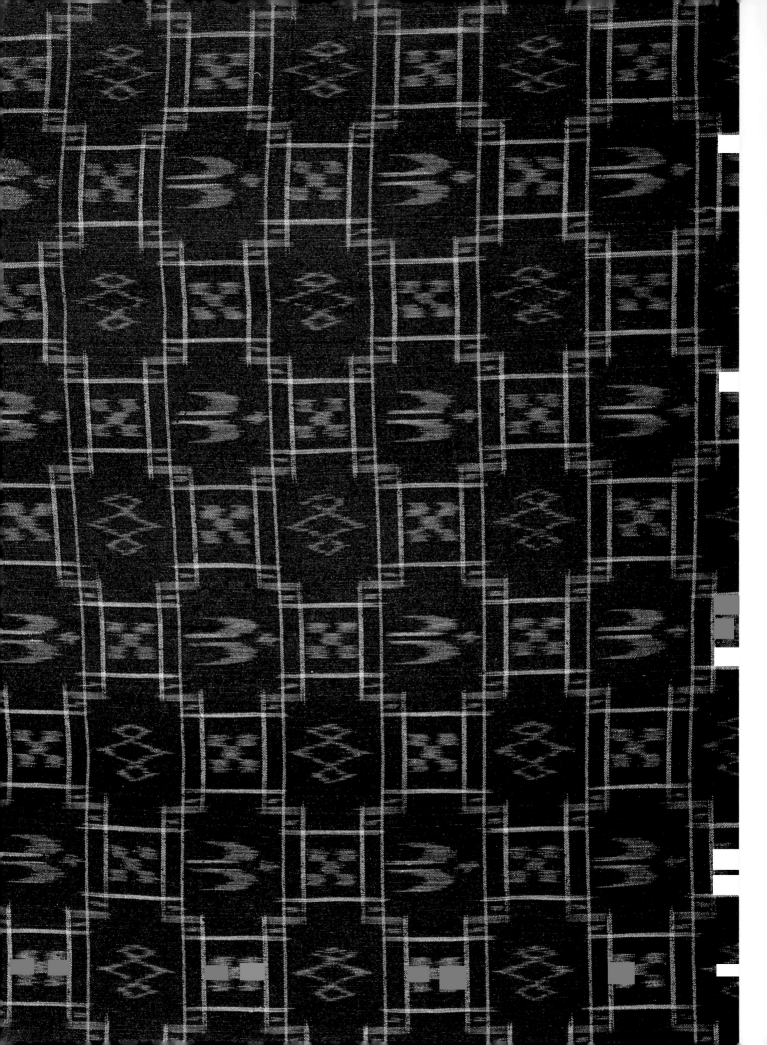

PREFACE

The emphasis of this book is on traditional methods of weaving, spinning and dyeing still in use today, but originating hundreds of years ago and passed down from one generation to another. In every case the equipment used is simple, but the methods of patterning are sometimes extremely complex, either at the dyeing stage before weaving commences or in the procedures used for the weaving itself. The textiles have been produced by people living in small communities often far removed from city life, initially for themselves but now bought by collectors who recognise their value.

I have selected eight subjects which I find of special interest: Navaho Indian weaving in North America; the work of the bedouin from the Arabian peninsula; the narrow-strip weaving of West Africa; inlay weaving in Nepal; Indonesian weaving, with special emphasis on the supplementary warp and weft weaves; *kasuri* resist dyeing of Japan; decorative weaves of Guatemala; and tapestry weaving in Peru.

The introduction describes the basic principles involved in the closely related, and interdependent, crafts of weaving, spinning and dyeing, in order to prepare the general reader for the more detailed descriptions that follow.

Each chapter starts with a brief geographical and historical sketch of the area, or country, in order to set the scene. This is followed by separate sections describing the spinning of yarns used; the dye plants and dyeing procedures; the loom or looms used; and the weaving techniques (with the exception of the chapter on *kasuri*, which concentrates on the methods of binding).

Silk kasuri *fabric from the Ryukyu Islands of Japan, with a repeat design of birds and lanterns within a geometrical motif.*

ACKNOWLEDGEMENTS

I would like especially to thank the staff of the Department of Ethnography in the British Museum (Museum of Mankind) for allowing me frequent access to textiles in their collection, and for unfailing help in both the students' room and library. I am also grateful to the Trustees of the British Museum for permission to reproduce their photographs. Many other museums have also allowed me to study their reserve collections, notably the Museum für Völkerkunde, Basle; the Gewerbemuseum, Basle; the Museum für Völkerkunde, Berlin; the Royal Tropical Institute, Amsterdam; the Victoria and Albert Museum, London; the Horniman Museum, London; the Royal Scottish Museum, Edinburgh; the Whitworth Art Gallery, Manchester, and the American Museum, Bath.

I am much indebted to Krystyna Deuss who let me study and photograph her extensive collection of textiles from Guatemala, and to Marianne Straub who also read the chapter on Guatemala, making helpful comments, and gave me permission to use her photos.

Gigi Crocker, on the bedouin, and Susi Dunsmore, on Nepal, were both unstinting in their help, reading and commenting on the text and providing many photographs. I am also most grateful to Alison Mitchell for allowing me to reproduce so many of her pictures taken in Japan; to Nancy Stanfield for her photos from Nigeria; to Jenny Balfour-Paul for those of indigo-dyeing in the Oman; to Veronica Johnston for those of spinning and weaving in Nepal; and Tony Tompson for those of preparations for dyeing and weaving in Indonesia.

My grateful thanks also go to James Reid of New York, for supplying the photo of a Huari shirt; and to Pauline Bottrill, Kate Olver, Rodrick Owen, Tony Shuffrey, Margaret Sowden and Mary Wharlow, all of whom have also contributed to the illustrations. A full list of picture credits appears at the end of the book.

Finally, I would like to thank the many friends who have supported me in countless ways throughout the writing of this book, in particular Eva Wilson, who also gave me permission to reproduce her drawings on pages 11 and 64; Margaret Cannon, who checked the botanical names and helped compile the index; Olga Olver, who read each chapter as it was written and gave me her non-specialist reactions; and Michael Seagroatt, who was very helpful with the compilation of the bibliographical sources.

INTRODUCTION

The loom

Weaving is the process of interlacing one set of threads, the warp, with another set, the weft, which is inserted at right angles to the warp. The loom is the means of keeping the warp threads under tension in parallel order, and the use of the loom, with its two sets of threads at right angles to each other, sets weaving apart from other methods of producing textiles, such as knitting, knotting or crochet.

To explain the working of the loom in a way that can be easily understood, various looms from different parts of the world will be described, some requiring little construction and few materials, others, such as the four-shaft foot loom, having a more complex construction. Should it be thought that the latter is superior to the simpler looms that came before, this is not the case. On the contrary, the paradox is that the simpler the loom, the more complex the work that can be carried out on it. In most cases the reasons for any developments in loom design were twofold: to make the work easier and to increase the speed with which it could be accomplished.

It is thought that weaving developed out of basket and mat making, in which relatively resistant plant materials are interlaced without the use of any special apparatus. However, in mat making in the past, when the strips of plant material were laid out in parallel order on the ground prior to interlacing with the other strips which were to cross them, the first set of strips may well have been tied to two parallel bars to keep them in order and stop them from changing position. If finer plant material was used to make cloth, the need to have the material streched under tension between two bars would have been even greater (Bühler, 1940).

1   The earliest illustration of a ground loom appears on the side of a flat bowl dated 4000 BC, found at Badari in Central Egypt and now in the Petrie Museum, University College, London. It shows the warp stretched out between two beams

Note Numbers in the margin refer to illustrations.

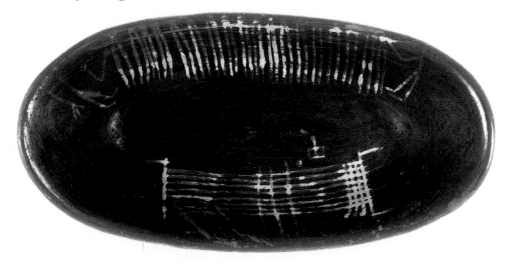

1 *Horizontal ground loom depicted on a bowl from Badari, Egypt, c.4000 BC. Petrie Museum, University College, London.*

2 A bedouin woman at work on a horizontal ground loom. Israel.

which are held in position by four pegs stuck in the ground, two at each end. A similar loom is depicted in a Middle Kingdom wall painting of the Eleventh Dynasty, two thousand years later. This same simple ground loom is still in use today in several parts of the world, but especially in the areas occupied by the 2 bedouin (see Chapter 2).

Warp threads may also be kept under tension in a vertical position by supporting a bar at each end with uprights, either on forked posts or lashed in position with ropes. The tension is produced by gathering groups of warp threads together and attaching them to weights in such a way that they hang just above ground level. This is known as the warp-weighted loom and appears in illustrations on Greek vases from the sixth to fourth centuries BC. It was also the 3 northern European loom and continued to be used in Scandinavia until early this century.

What appear to be loom weights have been found in archaeological sites in Egypt, but there is no other evidence to show that the warp-weighted loom was used there in ancient times. The vertical loom that did exist in Egypt, where a second bar takes the place of weights, appears in many wall paintings of the Twelfth Dynasty (c. 1900 BC), and shows weavers sitting at looms which are 4 similar to the tapestry and rug looms of today. The Navaho Indians of North America still use a simple vertical frame loom made from two upright posts with horizontal bars lashed to the top and bottom, as described in Chapter 1. Ancient Egyptian and Greek looms are described in detail in a book of that title by H. Ling Roth (1913).

The simplest loom, with a wide distribution on both sides of the Pacific, is neither horizontal nor vertical but something halfway between the two. This is 5 the back-strap, or body-tensioned loom, where the warp threads are wound around two bars, the far one of which is attached by a cord to a tree or post, and the near bar fitted with a comfortable strap to circle the weaver's hips. The warp threads lie at an angle of about 40° to the ground and the weaver has precise control of the tension of the threads through the movement of his or her body.

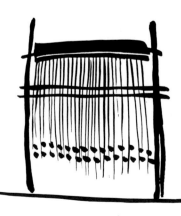

3 Warp-weighted loom from a scene on a black-figured skyphos (a deep cup), made in Boeotia, Greece, c.450–430 BC.

4 (left) *Vertical loom as depicted on the walls of tomb no. 104 at Thebes, Egypt. 18th Dynasty, c.1450–1425 BC.*

5 (below) *Back-strap loom in use in Guatemala.*

Before describing how the loom works, a thought must be given to how the warp threads are put in position on the loom. Warping, as the process of making a warp is called, can either take place directly on the loom, or separately around pegs and then transferred on to it. On the simple ground loom of the bedouin or the vertical loom of the Navaho, for example, the warp is wound directly on to two parallel beams, the distance between them determined by the length of the object to be woven. Two people squat, one at each end, with a ball of warp yarn to hand. The yarn is secured to one end of a beam and thrown to the person at the other end, who takes it over and under that beam and throws it back, and so on, forming a figure-of-eight as the threads form one plane mid-way between the two, known as the cross. This cross is of vital importance because it determines the order in which the threads are wound off should they get disturbed at any stage. 6

Longer warps are wound off on pegs stuck into the ground or protruding from walls. They can be positioned any distance apart, and are usually arranged in such a way that a cross can be made at both ends. When a sufficient number of threads have been wound off, the loops formed at each end where the warp circles the posts, together with the crosses, are all tied up with short lengths of yarn, after which the warp can be safely removed and wound on to a stick or chained (as in crochet) to reduce its length. Because of the crosses tied up at each end, the warp retains its parallel order when mounted on the loom. A warping board may also be used; this is a board with many pegs driven into it, so arranged that even long warps can be made in a small area. 7

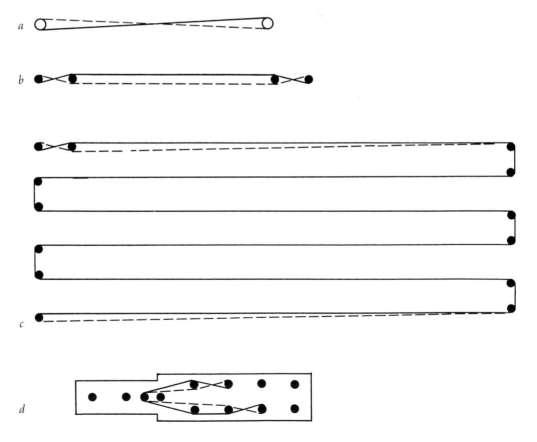

6 Different methods of laying a warp:
(a) a warp wound around two parallel beams (side view);
(b) a warp wound around four posts, forming a cross at each end;
(c) a very long warp (as made in West Africa, for example) wound around many posts set up in an open space, with a cross formed at the beginning only;
(d) the arrangement of posts on a Guatemalan warping bench, which allows for a variety of warps of differing lengths to be made.

So far, only the methods of making the warp and keeping the warp threads parallel and under tension once in position on the loom have been considered, but the loom has other important functions. How is the weft thread interlaced with the warp threads, for example? Presumably, in earliest times the weft was laboriously put in with the fingers, over and under each warp in turn. On the second row, the weft would go over the warps where previously it had gone under, and vice versa, a slow process indeed. If, however, the weft was wound on a long pointed stick, a shuttle (a grooved flat stick), or threaded on a long needle and inserted over and under several warp threads at a time, it must have become apparent that it would be possible to keep a flat stick or rod permanently in position, lifting up every alternate warp thread the full width of the warp, and that if turned on its edge this flat stick would leave a triangular space (which weavers call the shed) through which the weft could easily be passed.

If a shed stick lifted every even-numbered warp, why could not another stick be inserted to lift all the odd warps? The answer is that a second shed stick, if inserted in front of the first one, would negate its operation. One presumes, therefore, that the loom stayed at this stage of development, with one set of threads raised collectively by a stick or rod and the other set raised with the fingers, for some time before a far-reaching discovery was made.

This was that if individual loops are put around the warps lying underneath the shed stick or roll, and are then gathered up into little bunches, the lower layer of warp threads can be pulled up in groups unimpeded *between* the upper layer, producing a counter-shed. Alternatively, a continuous cord can be threaded under an odd-numbered warp and over a heddle bar, alternately over and under in sequence right across the width of the warp, so that lifting the heddle bar produces the counter-shed. The heddle bar lies in front of the shed stick, and by raising the shed stick and heddle bar alternately, a shed and counter-shed are made for inserting the weft, and weaving can proceed much more quickly. Once this fundamental development of the loom is grasped, the further developments, refinements or differences described throughout this book will be more easily understood.

At this stage, various methods were used, in addition to the tensioning of the loom, to ensure that the warp threads were kept parallel without crossing each other. Flat sticks, called lease sticks, were inserted, one under all the even warp threads and the other under the odd ones, just in front of the far beam, or warp beam. The tension produced between these two sticks kept the threads in order. Sometimes a cord took their place, or was twined between the threads in groups, and a few rows of plain weave inserted at the far end of the warp before the weaving commenced at the near end.

Another addition to the loom in some parts of the world was a device to keep the warp threads evenly spaced. This started as a comb-like piece of equipment with pegs set in a length of wood at intervals of half an inch (or 1 to 1.5 cm), but eventually fine slivers of reed — as many as twenty to the inch (eight to the centimetre) — came to be set upright in a frame. The whole tool was called the reed, but it did not really come into its own until it was encased in the batten as part of the foot loom, not yet described.

On some simple looms the functions of the heddle bar and the reed are combined in a rigid heddle, a tool in which the reeds or sticks used to separate the threads are pierced in the centre with a hole. The ends of the warp are threaded alternately through the space *between* the reeds and through a hole *in* the reed. When the reed is pushed down, it lowers the threads in the holes while the ones in the slits stay in the same position. When the heddle is raised, the opposite happens: these two movements produce the shed and the counter-shed.

Two more important developments were still to come: the first increased the length of cloth it was possible to weave, and the second increased the speed at which it could be woven. Up to this point the length of cloth had been restricted to the size of the loom, and although the warp was sometimes stretched out over a distance of many yards or metres on the ground loom, it was impractical to build enormously tall vertical frame looms. Roller beams therefore took the place of the original two bars – a warp beam for holding the excess warp, and a cloth beam on which to wind up the already woven cloth. As cloth was woven, warp was released from the warp beam and cloth wound on to the cloth beam, always maintaining the correct tension between the two.

The second important development was the introduction of foot treadles to operate the heddles heralding the treadle loom. Imagine the vertical loom, with its two rollers set about waist-height in a horizontal position, with legs to support the four corners and strengthened by cross bars at ground level. Instead

7

7 The simple Sherpa/Bhote horizontal foot loom as used in Nepal.

The art of the loom

of one heddle bar lifting one set of threads, two pairs of heddle bars work from both above and below, forming shafts that can be pulled up or down. The top pairs are connected by a pulley system hanging from a cross bar overhead, and the lower pairs by cords to treadles below. The simple vertical loom has now been converted into a horizontal treadle loom, using the feet to raise and lower the warp threads by depressing each treadle in turn, and leaving the hands free to pass the shuttle. The shuttle, too, changed to keep pace with the increase of speed which was now possible, the weft being wound around a hollow reed or paper core and threaded on to a wire contained within the cavity of a boat-shaped shuttle with could skim through the shed.

On the treadle loom, the reed, which has already been referred to, is set in a batten which either swings from a support overhead or pivots from the side supports below. This swinging batten containing the reed, has the added advantage of beating the weft thread, known as the pick, into position, a function previously accomplished with a smooth flat wooden tool known as the beater-in or sword.

8 *Man weaving on a horizontal foot loom, north-west of Lake Titicaca, Peru. The warp, weighted by a drag-stone, is similar in concept to West African methods.*

The treadle loom is still the tool of the hand-weaver in many parts of the world, but industry has long since dispensed with manpower to throw the shuttle and operate the treadles, substituting many alternative forms of energy in the constant search for increasing speed of production. But speed is not the concern of this book; on the contrary, it is the methods of production on the simplest of equipment, passed down from one generation to another with little change, that will be described. The interesting subject of the distribution of the various kinds of looms, and whether inventions were made simultaneously and independently on different continents or whether new ideas travelled from one continent to another, is left to anthropologists.

Spinning

The raw materials of textiles are the yarns from which they are woven, and, likewise, the raw materials of yarns are the fibres from which they are spun, for most, with the exception of reeled silk and certain leaves (for example, raffia), are made by twisting together separate fibres to make one continuous yarn. The natural fibres available fall mainly into two classes, animal and vegetable, though there is a smaller third group, mineral, which includes gold, silver, brass strips and asbestos. The animal group comprises on the one hand all the hair fibres, which include wool, and on the other the continuous filaments of silk. There are several sources of vegetable fibre, each from a different part of the plant, the fruit, stems, leaves or seeds.

Spinning is the process by which twist is imparted to a supply of overlapping fibres to make one continuous thread. In order to produce a carefully controlled supply of fibres, so that a smooth uniform thread can be spun, attention must be paid to this preparation. First, in the case of vegetable material, the fibres have to be extracted from the plant. The bast fibres of flax, hemp, jute, ramie and nettle are found in the stem, in bundles inside the outer layer, and in order to extract them the rest of the plant material has to be rotted away by a process known as retting. Bundles of plants are immersed in water until fermentation starts, at which point they are lifted out to drain. When the straw is completely dry, the unwanted parts are removed by processes known as breaking, scutching and combing; that is, breaking the outside bark, removing it and combing out the fibres. The leaf fibres of the agave plants, such as maguey, are treated in a similar way, as mentioned in Chapter 7 on Guatemala, and even the coconut, from which coir is obtained, is first immersed in sea-water for several months.

Cotton, the most widely used and versatile of all the vegetable fibres, consists of the seed-hairs of several species of *Gossypium*, plants belonging to the mallow family. The cotton plant grows in subtropical conditions, either on perennial trees and bushes or, more usually, on annual plants. The flowers bloom for a day, after which they fall off revealing the seed capsules, which, when fully matured burst open to reveal a mass of white fibres attached to the tightly packed seeds. The bolls, as the seed pods are called, have to be picked as soon as possible after opening, as the fibre will deteriorate if it is left on the bushes. After harvesting, the seeds have to be removed from the mass of cotton fibres, and the cotton prepared for spinning. There are slight variations from one country to another as to how this is done, as will become apparent in the individual descriptions.

The animal fibres, the best known of which is wool, are all animal hairs. People disagree as to whether the term 'wool' applies only to the hair of the domestic sheep, or whether it includes all hairs that are soft, flexible and characterised by their propensity to felting under certain conditions. The question arises in particular when referring to the soft undercoat of goats, as, for example, with cashmere, or the camel-like goats of South America, the llama, alpaca and vicuña, all of which have the characteristics of wool rather than hair.

The coat of the wild sheep, before domestication, consisted of stiff beard hairs on the surface and soft woolly hairs underneath, but by systematic breeding through the ages the sheep has been developed to produce only wool, although some stiffer hairs still persist. The camel and goat families, on the other hand, still combine the two types of hair.

The sheep's wool, or fleece as it is called, is sheared in the spring, the coat coming off in one piece. Among the other animals, some are sheared like the sheep, and others have the wool plucked from them at moulting time.

All the fibres mentioned so far have irregularities on the surface when seen under the microscope. Wool fibres have overlapping scales, similar to roof tiles, flax fibres have knots at intervals, and cotton fibres twist and turn, as a result of cell collapse. These characteristics are of great importance in facilitating the twisting of the fibres into a thread, as they provide cohesion. Before describing the process of spinning, however, reference must be made to that other important animal fibre, the smooth continuous filament of silk.

Silk, the most luxurious of all fibres, is obtained from the cocoon of the moth *Bombyx mori*. *Morus* is Latin for mulberry, and it is on the leaves of the mulberry tree that the silkworms, with their ravenous appetite, feed. When the cater-pillar is full grown and ready to spin a cocoon for itself, it emits silk from two orifices on its lower lip, two continuous strands united by a gelatinous substance called sericin. Inside the cocoon the caterpillar completes its metamorphosis into a moth, and if left in the wild would then break out, destroying the cocoon in the process. In sericulture, the chrysalis is stifled before it emerges, enabling the silk to be reeled off from several cocoons at the same time, because a single filament would be too delicate. The gum is loosened by floating the cocoons in hot water.

9

9 *Silk being reeled off from several cocoons as a preliminary to throwing.*

The reeled silk is then thrown, which is the term used for twisting it. The short filaments of waste silk and the silk from wild silkworms, such as the tussah moth, are spun in a similar fashion to wool and cotton, making a light and warm, but less lustrous, yarn. The production of silk is described in detail in Chapter 5.

As in tracing the origins of the loom, a certain amount of guesswork is involved when considering the early beginnings of spinning. In the case of plant material, generally considered the first to be used, it is possible that when baskets made of flax or similar plants began to rot, the fibres lying within the stems were revealed, suggesting a much finer source of supply which could perhaps be used for clothing (Ryder, 1968, p. 77). But these fine fibres would have no strength in them unless given some twist. In the case of wool, the same author suggests that the locks that form naturally in fleece became twisted into strands as they grew longer, suggesting the process of spinning.

If a handful of any fibres, held loosely, is gradually pulled out with the other hand and twisted between the thumb and fingers, a rudimentary thread is made.

10 *A bedouin man spinning wool with his hands prior to winding it on to a stick. Oman.*

Let go of this thread, however, and the whole thing immediately untwists. It is therefore necessary to wind the yarn on to a stick immediately after it has been
10 twisted. The stick then became a tool to help in the spinning process, because it was found that, if the yarn spiralled off the tip of it at a slight angle, while the stick was rolled down the thigh, the twist would flip off the end of it and run up into the drafted fibres. At the same time, these fibres would be pulled out from the mass held in the hand in sufficient quantity for the thickness of yarn being made. The real breakthrough came when a weight, pierced by a hole, was added to the stick in the form of a disc of stone, wood or clay which acted as a fly wheel, sustaining the momentum of the twirled stick, at the same time leaving both hands free to attend to the drafting of the fibres. Once such a weight, known as a whorl, was added to the shaft, making a spindle, the way was left open for the spinner to stand or walk with it freely rotating – the method referred to as 'drop-and-spin' – or sit, supporting the spindle in a bowl, the method used for delicate cotton fibres.

The spindle was the principal spinning tool for thousands of years, and is still
11 used in many parts of the world. Spindles vary considerably in size: short, fine, delicate fibres are spun with a lightweight version, about $\frac{1}{8}$ in in diameter (3 mm), and 6 to 8 in long (15 to 20 cm), with a tiny pottery whorl; while, at the other extreme, a large wooden spindle, with a shaft 18 in or more (45 cm) in length, with a wooden whorl, is used by the Navaho for spinning wool. The position of

11 Carding and spinning wool: three generations at the cottage in Pakhribas, Koshi Hills, Nepal.

the whorl in relation to the shaft also varies: it is sometimes placed at the top, sometimes the bottom and sometimes the middle of the shaft and is not always circular, since in areas of the Middle East two crossed bars placed at the top of the shaft take the place of the whorl. The shaft is usually tapered at one end, and blunt at the other, and often has a notch near the top of the blunt end in which a half hitch in the yarn can be secured to keep the spinning spindle in an upright position. The spindle with crossed bars is topped with a screw for the same purpose. An ancient Egyptian wooden spindle has a groove spiralling up towards the end to keep the yarn in position.

Before spinning can commence, a length of spun yarn is attached to the shaft, close to the whorl, spiralling up to the tip. The prepared fibres are held loosely in the left hand and the spindle is held in the right. By a twist between the fingers and thumb the spindle is set turning and allowed to drop, while the left hand draws the fibres away from the right hand which, after dropping the spindle, moves to controlling the amount of twist allowed into the drafting zone (the area between the prepared fibres and the yarn where the drawing out of the fibres takes place). The weight of the suspended spindle helps in the drafting process as well as in the twisting which follows. When the spindle reaches the ground, the yarn has to be unhitched from the point of the shaft, carefully wound into a cone shape with its base against the whorl, and spiralled up to the point, ready for the whole cycle of drafting and attenuating, followed by twisting, followed by winding on, to repeat itself.

The introduction of the spinning wheel is generally accepted to have taken place in India between AD 500 and AD 1000 (Born, 1939, p. 989). The spindle with its whorl, in the shape of a flat disc with a groove in the rim, rests in bearings horizontally between two upright posts set fairly close on either side of the whorl. The posts are set at one end of a plank, on the other end of which two taller posts support a large wheel by its axle, one end of which is extended to

12 *A bedouin woman spinning with a suspended spindle* (left), *and drawing the fibres upwards with her left hand* (right). *Oman.*

13   form a handle. The Indian wheel, like others in the Far East, was rimless, the two sets of spokes being connected at their points by a network of cords on which the driving band ran. The band on the wheel also ran in the groove on the spindle, so that when the handle was turned the spindle rotated at great speed due to the differential between the diameter of the two. The wheel was not such a breakthrough as one might imagine since spinning was still divided into the separate stages of drafting, twisting and winding on. It did, however, perform another function which it could do far faster than was possible by hand – that of winding bobbins of yarn.

It was not until the invention of a flyer attached to the spindle (a U-shaped piece of wood with hooks on, that circled a separately rotating bobbin on the spindle shaft), and a treadle attached to the wheel to provide foot power, that yarn could be spun and wound on continuously without interruption. For speed this was a great advance on the hand spindle and spindle wheel, and was used in Europe in the houses of both rich and poor from the Middle Ages until the Industrial Revolution. However, this did not dislodge the use of the hand spindle in other parts of the world. This is not surprising when one compares spinning on a simple tool that can be taken on any journey and combined with other tasks with a rather complex piece of apparatus with many moving parts, which necessitates a settled way of life, not to mention capital outlay.

13 The woman on the left is spinning cotton on a six-spoked rimless spinning wheel, while the woman on the right is bowing the cotton fibres; between them stands the cotton gin which separates the fibres from the seeds. Indonesia.

Dyeing

The natural materials from which yarns are spun already include a variety of shades. For daily use these would suffice, but man has always loved bright colours, and the search for colouring substances other than natural fibre colour began in prehistory and continues to the present day, as evidenced by the vast chemical dye industries. However, a large range of colours was available to the dyer before the discovery of the first synthetic dye in 1858, as can be seen by looking at textiles prior to that date.

Primitive man discovered juices in plants and colouring substances in the earth and applied them with sticks to their bodies or to rudimentary cloth, but these were only temporary applications and were easily brushed off. They did not therefore constitute dyeing, whereby the colour forms a permanent bond with the fibre, usually in the presence of water in a prepared dye bath. This was a more sophisticated concept developed in the ancient civilised centres of the world – India, China, Egypt, Mexico, Peru, Greece and Rome – where dyeing became a specialised trade. From these cultural centres dyeing methods spread farther afield, and were often adopted by women as an extension of their many other small-scale domestic activities.

Modern scientific works divide existing dyeing methods into three classes, according to whether the natural colouring matter dyes directly (substantive dyes) or requires an auxillary agent to precipitate it on the fabric (vat and mordant dyes) (Bühler, 1948, p. 2488).

SUBSTANTIVE DYES

Substantive dyes are the simplest to prepare as they are made from substances that dissolve and give their colour readily to water, and dye directly without the need of further additions. With some of these dyes, the fibres simply absorb the colour and consequently are not very fast to light or washing, but with others a chemical reaction takes place between the dye and the fibre, making a permanent colour.

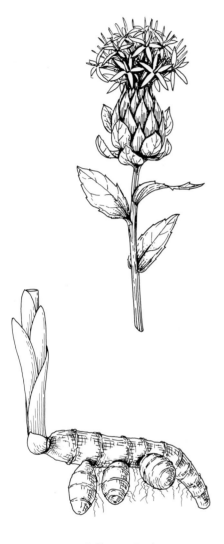

14 (top) *Safflower* (Carthamus tinctorius).

15 (above) *Turmeric, the* Curcuma *rhizome.*

The substantive dyes are a small group, but include flowers, roots, fruit and lichens. Safflower (*Carthamus tinctorius*) was used many centuries before the birth of Christ in both Persia and the Far East. The flowers contain two separate colouring matters, a water-soluble yellow and an insoluble red. The yellow dissolves in soft water and was used for dyeing the yellow robes of Buddhist monks; the remaining red insoluble matter has to be extracted by working in an alkaline bath after which it is neutralised with acid. It was used for dyeing legal 'red tapes' long after better reds became available (Ponting, 1980, p. 157).   14

Turmeric comes from the *Curcuma* rhizome. When crushed to a fine powder, it dissolves in water and dyes cotton fabrics a strong yellow, though the colour is not fast to washing or light. It has been in use since ancient times in India, one of the oldest centres of dyeing, and through trade spread to east and west.   15

Annatto is the name of the dye obtained from the fleshy pulp around the seed of *Bixa orellana*, a native plant of Central and South America. It was used for dyeing silk and produces a bright orange, but, like turmeric, is fugitive and fades in the light.   16

Perhaps it is worth mentioning, on the question of fugitive colours, that whereas the transitory nature of the colour appears to modern eyes in the twentieth century as a distinct drawback, in more primitive societies dyeing with a substantive dye was no more arduous than washing, and the cloth would from time to time simply be re-dipped, especially prior to a festival or some other special occasion.

From the more temperate zones there are several woods or barks that dye animals fibres yellow or brown. Barberry (*Berberis vulgaris*) produces yellow, and the bark of the oak (*Quercus* species) creates a dark brown, the tannin in the bark helping to make the colour fast. Walnuts, as well as other parts of *Juglans* species, are used in many parts of the world for their browns.

A large group of substantive dyes comes from lichens. Lichens are not like other plants, in that they are formed from two distinct, dissimilar organisms, a fungus and an alga, living together in a mutually beneficial relationship (symbiosis). They are described as being either foliose, crustaceous or fruticose, and are found growing on rocks, walls, buildings or trees. They are sensitive to pollution and take a long time to grow, so people anxious to protect their native plants are now reluctant to use them for dyeing. This was not so in the past, however, when vast quantities were gathered in the northern parts of the British Isles, Iceland, the Scandinavian countries and North America, as well as on the shores of the Mediterranean and the Canary Islands.

Lichens contain colouring matter in the form of colourless acids, and in some cases they need only to be broken up, if dry, or bruised, if fresh, and boiled in water to produce colours in the dye bath. Either the wool to be dyed is layered with the lichens in the dye bath, or the colour is first extracted from the plants and the water strained off into the bath and used for dyeing. These are known as 'boiling water' lichens and are very simple to use. Orchil and cudbear were substantive dyes commercially produced in the past from various species of lichen. Orchil was made from *Rocella tinctoria* and other kinds found growing in the Canary Islands and the Azores. The plant material was reduced to a pulp with water and ammonia and allowed to ferment for from two to three weeks (Mairet, 1952, p. 18). Cudbear was made from *Ochrolechia tartarea* and other kinds in the Shetland Islands and Western Highlands of Scotland.

Lichens make a fascinating subject for study, and references and recipes will be found in many books on dyes, but *Lichens for Vegetable Dyeing* by Eileen Bolton deals exclusively with the subject.

16 Bixa orellana. *The dye annatto is obtained from the fleshy pulp around the seed.*

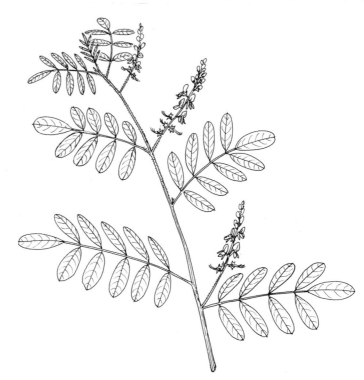

17 Indigofera tinctoria, *from which indigo is extracted.*

VAT DYES

Certain dye substances do not dissolve in water, but are transformed into water-soluble compounds in an alkaline solution. During this process the oxygen is removed, allowing the dye to penetrate the fibres. The dye then becomes permanently fixed by subsequent oxidation in the air.

Indigo is one such dye, with a distribution across India, Indonesia, China, Japan, Africa and Central and South America. Indigo is the name of the colouring matter, rather than the plant, and is obtained from about fifty plants, including *Indigofera tinctoria.* It is present in the leaves of the plants in the form of a colourless glucoside called indican, and is extracted from the plants in a process of fermentation:

17

19

First the plants are cut just as they mature, then steeped and allowed to ferment; next the solution containing indigotin [indican] is drawn off and the plants are disposed of; the indigotin is then subjected to another series of steps. The solution is beaten with paddles to incorporate air into it and to promote oxidation. When oxidation is complete, the indigo, pressed, cut, and dried, is ready for market. (Adrosko, 1968, p. 17.)

18

In order to use the indigo thus obtained it has once again to be fermented and reduced in an alkaline bath, the ingredients of which vary from country to country, if not village to village, according to what is available locally. Fermenting ingredients may include madder or other plants, honey, dates, grapes or bran, for example, with lime or potash as the alkali. Jill Goodwin (1982, p. 69) describes stale urine as the perfect reducing agent:

The bacteria in urine require oxygen for survival which they obtain from urea, and in the course of their life cycle they liberate hydrogen which converts the indigo to white. At this stage the ammonia in urea provides the necessary alkali for dissolving the indigo white, and after at least two weeks have been allowed for fermentation the yarn may be soaked in the solution and aired and permanent blue indigo will be deposited on the fibres.

Today synthetic indigo, first marketed in 1897 and identical in structure to natural indigo (though lacking the trace materials present in the plant material), is made in vast quantities. So too are easily managed and stable reducing agents, making it possible to satisfy the world market for blue jeans and overalls of a colour which seems to have a universal appeal and is at the same time fast to light and washing, although not impervious to rubbing.

19 *Indigo fields, Ibri, Oman.*

Northern Europe also had a source of indigo in the woad plant *Isatis tinctoria*. This contained the same colouring matter as *Indigofera* but in considerably smaller amounts, which meant that larger quantities of plant material were needed to obtain the same quantity of indigo. Nevertheless, it was an important dye in medieval times and, although it was eventually ousted by the newly arrived indigo from the East, it continued in use, sometimes as an ingredient of the new indigo vat dye, until early in the twentieth century.

Another colourless dye relying on oxygen, and in this case sunlight as well, to convert it to colour is the ancient Tyrean, or imperial, purple. It is found in liquid form in a gland of the *purpura* shellfish, species of whelks. As is well known, this purple colour was highly esteemed by the Romans, who initially only allowed it to be used to dye the robes worn by high officials, although later it was to become a more general fashion. What is perhaps less well known is the wide distribution of purpura fishing and dyeing, not only in many other countries around the Mediterranean, but also across the Atlantic in Mexico, Guatemala and Peru. In coastal areas around the Mediterranean huge mounds of discarded shells indicate where the large dyeing centres were located; whereas in Central and South America the juice is extracted by blowing on the gland or by rubbing two whelks together, in both cases stimulating the gland that excretes the dye but not destroying the source.

A full account of imperial purple can be found in K. G. Ponting's *A Dictionary of Dyes and Dyeing*, based on *CIBA Review*, Vol. 4, which is devoted to 'Purple'.

MORDANT DYES

20 Mordant dyes are by far the largest group. Mordants form a link between the molecules of the fibre and the dye, making a bond between the two, with the result that strong and more or less permanent colours are made from dye materials which, in the absence of a mordant, would be pale or non-existent.

Mordants are metal salts, and may be found as natural deposits in the ground, dissolved in mud or as soluble compounds in certain plants. In the form of chemical salts, they are dissolved in water and the fibres, yarns or cloth given a preliminary boiling in the solution; alternatively, the mordant is added to the dye bath so that mordanting and dyeing take place simultaneously; or the mordanting is done after the dyeing has taken place, either in a separate bath or added to the dye bath towards the end of dyeing. The Navahos and the bedouin, for example, who live where water is a scarce commodity, use the 'all-in-one-bath' method, but where there is an ample supply of water the mordanting is often done as a preliminary treatment. For dark colours the mordanting can be done afterwards, 'saddening' the colour. When several different shades of the same colour are wanted, differently mordanted yarns can all be put in the same pot together, but on removal will be seen to be different hues, each mordant having modified the colour in a different way.

20 Mordant-dyed yarns hanging out to dry. From left: pine cones, onion skins, madder, cochineal and weld.

ARTICLES.	PRICES.		PER.	OBSERVATIONS.
ASHES, Montreal, Pot	23s 0d @ 24	0	Cwt.	About 200 brls. Montreal Pot **ASHES** have disposed of this week at lower rates, viz. 24 new and 23s for old; also 100 brls. Pearl at We reduce our quotations accordingly.
Pearl....	31 0 , 32	0	,,	
ANNATTO, Flag.........	1 4 , 1	6	lb.	10 casks Annatto sold at 1s 5d @ 1s 7d; the l price now demanded for good quality.
ARGOL,				
Red, Oporto, Naples, &c ..	33 0 , 40	0	Cwt.	No actual sales have occurred in Argol, but sev parcels of importance have been forwarded into interior.
Florence, Bologna, &c.	42 0 , 46	0	,,	
White.. do ......do......	43 0 , 52	0	,,	
Naples, French, &c..	36 0 , 44	0	,,	
BARK, Quercitron, N.York &c.	18 0 , 20	0	,,	Only small lots of Quercitron Bark have been so 18s @ 20s.
Philadel ..	20 0 , 21	0	,,	
BERRIES, Persian, good ..£	21 0 , 22	0	,,	No sales reported in Yellow Berries.
ord. & mid.	17 0 , 19	0	,,	
Turkey	6 15 , 7	5	,,	Brimstone has been in good demand, and upwar 1300 tons have changed hands, viz. about 200 ordinary third quality at £9 12s 6d from the c 1100 tons second quality at £10 10s @ £10 12 and 50 tons first quality, in small lots, at £11.
BRIMSTONE, Sicily, Rough	10 10 , 11	5	Ton.	
Tuscan	11 10 , 12	0	,,	
COCHINEAL, Black, dty.pd.	6s 3 , 6	6	lb.	
Silver	5 7 , 6	0	,,	Dull.
CREAM TARTAR, Venetian	70 0 , 72	0	Cwt.	A few casks Cream Tartar sold at 70s @ 72s.
French .	None.		,,	
Brown .	52 0 , ———		,,	
Yellow .	60 0 , ———		,,	
DYEWOODS,				
BARWOOD, Angola......£	8 10 , 10	0	Ton	
Gaboon	5 10 , 7	10	,,	
CAMWOOD	19 10 , 24	0	,,	Logwood this week has experienced a further dec of 15s @ 20s per ton, 100 tons Campeachy ha been sold at £9 10s @ £10, and 120 tons Jam at £7 @ £7 12s 6d. The transactions in o descriptions of **DYEWOODS** consist chiefl about 60 tons Fustic,—Jamaica £13 5s and T pico £12 @ £13.
FUSTIC, Spanish	12 10 , 13	0	,,	
Ceara	12 15 , 13	0	,,	
Tampico	12 0 , 13	0	,,	
Cuba	16 0 ,		,,	
LOGWOOD, Jamaica	7 0 , 7	10	,,	
Honduras	8 0 , 8	10	,,	
Campeachy ..	9 10 ,		,,	
NICARAGUA WOOD, Solid.	11 0 , 14	0	,,	
Small	7 0 , 8	0	,,	
LIMA, middling to good ..	15 10 , 16	10	,,	
inferior	11 0 , 14	0	,,	
GUM, Senegal .... duty pai	67 0 , 68	0	Cwt.	No sales reported in Gum. Sales of East India a damaged Senegal are advertised for Wednesd next.
Gedda	58 0 , 60	0	,,	
E.I. good & fine, in bd.	50 0 , 54	0	,,	
ordinary & mid ..	20 0 , 45	0	,,	
OIL, OLIVE, Gallipoli, direct	52 10 , 53	0	Tun of 252	Not more than 20 tuns Olive **OIL** have been sol Portugal £46 10s @ £48 10s, Trieste £50.. Small parcels of Palm Oil sold at £39.
Trieste	50 0 , 51	0		
Sicily	50 0 ,		Impert. gallons	
Malaga	43 0 , ———			
Portugal & Seville	47 0 , 48	0	,,	
Levant	47 0 , 49	0	,,	
PALM	39 0 , ———		Ton	
TALLOW, Russian........	48s 0 , 49	0	Cwt.	Not much doing in Tallow. Some P. Y. C. sold 48s 6d ex ship, and 49s required in store.
Buenos Ayres, &c	43 0 , 46	0	,,	
SHUMAC, Malaga, new....	None.		,,	The sales in Shumac consist of 250 bags Palermo 12s 9d @ 13s, and 94 bags Messina, damage at 8s.
Sicily	12 0 , 13	0	,,	
Verona	9 0 , 9	6	,,	
Trieste	9 6 , 10	0	,,	
GALLS, Turkey, white .. £	3 3 , 3	5	,,	In Galls no transactions are reported.
mixed	3 10 ,		,,	
blue	3 15 , 4	0	,,	
LAC DYE, middling to good.	1s 2 , 4	0	lb.	A few chests Lac Dye sold at 11d.
ordin. & inferior.	0 9 , 1	1	,,	
SHELL LAC, Orange, in bd.	85 0 , 120	0	Cwt.	No sales reported in Shell Lac. 150 chests to offered by auction next week.
Liver & Block	55 0 , 70	0	,,	
SALTPETRE, E. India, d. p.	26 0 , 30	0	,,	The business done in Saltpetre has been confined small parcels at previous rates. 500 bags Nitra of Soda have been disposed of at 14s 6d @ 15s
Peruvian	15 6 , 16	0	..	

Imports of **DRYSALTERIES, WOOL, &c** *from 21st to 27th June inclusive.*

			Imports 1st J
56 casks Annatto	139 casks Trieste Oil	38 chests East India Indigo	
81 , Argol	15 , Malaga do.	100 serons Spanish do.	
91 , New York Bark	15 , Portugal do.	22 casks Dutch Madder	
205 tons Brimstone	443 , Palm do.	70 bales Naples Roots	Foreign.
334 serons Cochineal	681 , Russian Tallow	622 bags Spanish Madder	Scotch .
17 casks Cream Tartar	136 , Monte Video do.	123 , Scotch Wool	Irish ...
126 tons Fustic	730 bags Sicily Shumac	43 , English do.	English .
62 , Jamaica Logwood	2350 , Trieste do.	113 , Irish do.	
19 , St. Domingo do.	11 chests Lac Dye	56 , German do.	
558 , Campeachy do.	225 , Shell Lac	108 , Italian do.	
1398 bags Gum Senegal	1953 bags Saltpetre	919 , N. S. Wales do.	
26 chests do. Arabic			

21 *Price list giving information about the trade in dyes in the first half of the nineteenth century.*

ARTICLES.	PRICES.	PER.
GO, *in bond*,		
le, ord. & mid.	3s 9 @ 5s 0	lb.
good & fine	5 6 , 6 3	,,
gal, ord. & mid. consg }	6 6 , 7 9	,,
copper & violet.. }		
good and fine ditto.	8 0 , 8 6	,,
do. vio. & purp. vio.	8 9 , 9 3	,,
do. purple and blue	9 3 , 9 6	,,
dras	*None.*	
timala, Cortes, *in bond*	3 6 , 5 0	,,
Sobres	5 3 , 6 9	,,
Flora	7 0 , 7 6	,,
acca, Cortes	4 3 , 5 6	,,
Sobres	5 9 , 6 9	,,
Flora	7 0 , 7 6	,,
DER, Dutch. Crop....	70 0 , 80 0	Cwt.
Ombro..	58 0 , 68 0	,,
Gamene..	40 0 , 50 0	,,
Mull..	10 0 , 25 0	,,
ench, E X F F.......	68 0 , ——	,,
E S F & E S F F	62 0 , 64 0	,,
S F F	52 0 , 56 0	,,
S F	48 0 , 50 0	,,
nish	*None.*	,,
DER ROOTS, Turkey.	45 0 , 47 0	,,
French.	47 0 , ——	,,
Naples, Syrian, &c..	36 0 , 38 0	,,
LOWER, Bengal, *in ba.*		
od and fine ....£	7 0 , 7 0	,,
dinary and middling ..	2 10 , 4 10	,,
bay, *duty paid*	1 5 , 2 0	,,
L, Highland Laid	12 0 , ——	Stone.
White ...	14 6 , 15 0	of
oway, Laid & fine cross.	14 0 , 16 6	24 *lbs.*
viot White	30 0 , 34 0	,,
Washed	20 0 , 28 0	,,
Laid and cross ..	14 0 , 18 0	,,
tch, Skin	0 4½, 1 0	lb.
lish Fleeces, Dorset, }	1 6 , 1 8	,,
ilts, &c. .... }		
kin, old, combing.....	1 4 , ——	,,
o. short	0 10 , 1 6	,,
h Fleeces, comb & Hoggett	1 6 , 1 7	,,
Wedder	1 4½, 1 6	,,
man Fleeces	2 2 , 3 0	,,
Lambs'	2 0 , 2 9	,,
Skin....	1 4 , 2 0	,,
ssian Zegay	1 1½, 1 3½	,,
Donsky.........	0 9 , 0 9½	,,
Lambs'.........	0 7½, 0 9½	,,
ssa, fine	2 0 , 3 6	,,
can, Smyrna, & Italian .		
nwashed	0 6 , 0 6¼	,,
Washed	0 9 , 0 11	,,
nish R and R R	2 3 , 2 9	,,
F S A	1 6 , 2 0	,,
tugal R and R R......	1 4 , 1 8	,,
F A S	0 10 , 1 4	,,
South Wales Fleece...	1 6 , 2 6	,,
Lamb ...	1 8 , 2 3	,,
t India	0 4½, 0 10	,,
nos Ayres	0 7 , ——	,,
key Goats' Mohair	1 4 , 1 6	,,
yrna Black	0 4 , 0 7	,,
key White	0 8½, 0 11	,,

OBSERVATIONS.

The very limited supply of **INDIGO** on the market prevents transactions worthy of notice.

There is rather more inquiry for **MADDER**, without any business of importance having been done.

No transactions in any description of Madder Roots reported in the general market.

A few bales Bengal Safflower sold at 90s per cwt.

The attention of the Trade being directed to the London sale of **WOOL** to take place at the end of next week, and to the collection of the English clip, the business doing in the article here is on a very limited scale, and only trifling parcels find buyers as wanted for immediate consumption.

The "Laura" arrived from Sydney, N. S. Wales on Wednesday last, with 919 bales. Other vessels are shortly expected, when a sale will be announced in about a month.

ool, from June.	38.	1839.
	ags	Bags
	07	38521
	24	3497
	15	2153
	80	737

SALES ADVERTISED.

Saturday, 29th June.
40 tons Jamaica Logwood
Wednesday, 3d July.
333 chests Gum Arabic
27 , do. Animi
158 , Shell Lac

134 chests Lac Dye
214 bags Seed Lac
45 casks Dutch and French Madder
800 bags Messina Shumac
490 , Sicily do.

26 serons Guatimala Indigo
4 chests Bengal do.
13 serons Cochineal
149 casks Argol
553 bags damag'd Gum Senegal
100 bales do. Madder Roots.

EDWARDS, DANSON & CO.
Brokers.

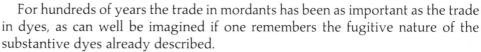

For hundreds of years the trade in mordants has been as important as the trade in dyes, as can well be imagined if one remembers the fugitive nature of the substantive dyes already described.

Alum, one of the oldest mordants, opened up the possibilities of dyeing a whole range of permanent reds and yellows. Cochineal and madder, two red dyes with an ancient history, are used in several of the areas discussed in the following chapters; this is especially true of madder, still in use, not only in its cultivated form as *Rubia tinctoria* but in the many other species of the genus *Rubia*, which have a wide distribution across the continents.

Plants that produce yellow are legion, each part of the world having its particular favourites. The most important yellow in the northern hemisphere is weld, *Reseda luteola*, which gives a strong yellow on alum (potassium aluminium sulphate), an old gold on chrome (potassium dichromate), an acid yellow on tin (stannous chloride), and a deep olive to brown on iron (ferrous sulphate).

These metal salts, so conveniently available for sale in modern societies, have to be sought in the environment by others. Natural deposits of alum are found in certain parts of the world, and much use is made of iron springs and mud. Some plants contain soluble compounds of aluminium; and others contain tannin which also acts as a mordant. Vinegar or citrus fruits, salt, stale urine and lye (alkaline water made by soaking burnt vegetable ashes) are other mordants likely to be at hand.

23

22

22 (above) *Weld* (Reseda luteola).

23 (right) *Madder:* Rubia tinctoria *(left);* R. cordifolia *(right).*

24 (below) *Brazil wood* (Caesalpina echinata).

Many of the wood dyes are mordant dyes, traded in the form of logs or chips, particularly from South America: fustic (*Chlorophora tinctoria*) and quercitron (*Quercus velutina*) for yellows; logwood (*Haematoxylon campechianum*) for mauves, greys and black; and brazil wood (*Caesalpinia echinata* and others) for light reds. Brazil, the country, was in fact named after the colour (and not the other way around as might be expected), as the wood had been used as a dye in the East long before related species were discovered growing on the South American continent.

In a short introductory chapter such as this it has only been possible to draw attention to some of the natural dye materials. The discovery of chemical dyes in the middle of the nineteenth century spread to even the remotest parts, quickly taking the place of natural dyes. This is not surprising when one considers that one tiny box or tin holding a few ounces of dye powder can quickly be converted into a dye bath with the simple addition of boiling water; a procedure which had previously taken hours or even days, now accomplished in minutes. But there are places in the world — for example Indonesia — where the actual process of dyeing using plants and recipes handed down from one generation to another is of the utmost significance and part of the ritual, and where the length of time taken is of no account. Here dyeing continues in the same time-honoured way.

25 Synthetic colours used in a man's shawl from Guatemala: face and reverse of the intricate pattern area.
Private collection.

In other countries, for example Peru, where the blues of indigo, the reds and pinks of cochineal, and the yellows, browns and black of plants and trees gave way to vivid oranges, mauves, turquoises, emeralds and other synthetic dyes, the pendulum shows signs of swinging back again. Changes are occurring partly in response to the demands of sophisticated tourists who have tired of the bright colours and ask for textiles woven from yarns which have been dyed from natural dyes, and partly as a result of the Indians' new awareness of their heritage. They are learning once again how to use their indigenous plants.

Weaving

To weave is to form a textile by interlacing two sets of threads. The active element, the weft, is passed through the passive element, the warp, held taut on the loom, row by row until the textile is complete. The function of the loom and the devices for separating the threads into two layers to facilitate passing the weft from one selvedge to the other have already been described, but the manner in which the threads interlace has not. This section classifies the different types of interlacement, naming the different textile structures and suggesting the possible reasons for selecting one structure rather than another.

Plain weaving, also called tabby, is the simplest and most frequently used of all structures. The weft interlaces the warp threads in single units, over one, under one, etc. in the first row, and under those where previously it had gone over, and vice versa, in the next. Another way of putting it is: in rows one, three, five, and so on, all the odd-numbered threads are lifted, and in rows two, four, and six, all the even-numbered threads are lifted. 26

Simple as this arrangement of interlacement is, the resulting textiles vary considerably because not only does each different fibre or yarn used give the resulting cloth a different look and feel, but the spacing of the warp threads in relation to the weft completely alters its character.

When the same yarn is used, and there are the same number of threads to the inch or centimetre, in both warp and weft, the resulting cloth is called balanced plain weave. However, when the warp threads are crammed together, so that the weft is hardly, or no longer, visible, the resulting cloth is called warp-faced plain 27 weave. Likewise, if the warp threads are spaced out so that successive weft threads are not held apart, as they are in balanced weave, but completely cover the warp, the result is weft-faced plain weave. This is the form of plain weaving 28 used in many rugs and most tapestries. 29

26 (left) *Balanced plain weave: 'tabby'.*

27 (centre) *Warp-faced plain weave.*

28 (right) *Weft-faced plain weave.*

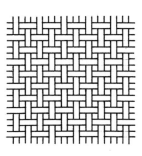
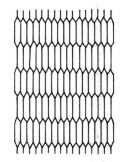
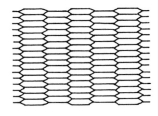

The art of the loom

Not only is the surface of the textile altered by the choice of yarn and the density of the warp, but the effect of coloured yarns is also altered. One popular way of adding colour to plain weave fabrics is to introduce stripes into the warp or weft, or both. If the same sequence of coloured stripes is used in both warp and weft in a balanced plain weave cloth, the result is a check or gingham (from the Malay word *gingang*, meaning striped). Examine a gingham carefully and you will find that if two colours are used, for example black and white, alternately in stripes of equal width, the finished cloth will be checked in black, white and grey, the grey being made when white weft crosses black warp, or black weft crosses white warp. Following on from this, if black warp stripes on a white ground are woven with a white weft in a balanced plain weave, the result will not be black, but grey stripes on white. (And if black were used instead of white for the weft, the result would be black stripes on a grey ground.) Neither way would the result be black on white.

Using colour on a warp- or weft-faced plain weave, rather than a balanced weave, therefore gives one the possibility of using colours at their full strength and not modified by the colour of the weft or warp respectively. Hence many fabrics with the stripes running down the length of the warp tend to be warp-faced, and tapestry, with its infinite possibilities for colourful designs, and horizontally striped fabrics are weft-faced.

29 *Weft-faced plain weave: detail of a Navaho blanket. British Museum.*

31

30

30 *A weft-faced cotton textile from Niger, West Africa. British Museum.*

31 (facing page) *West African narrow-strip cloth from Nigeria: plain, striped and checked strips have been sewn together. British Museum.*

An extension of plain weave alters the number of threads in the unit, for example weaving over and under two warp threads. If the weft insertion is also repeated so that not only the warp threads but also the weft work in pairs, the balanced plain weave commonly known as basket weave results. There are other extensions of plain weave with different numbers of warp or weft threads interlacing, but as long as the intersection of warp and weft remains over-one-under-one, albeit in groups, the construction is plain weave, and the textile can be woven on any loom with two lifting devices, one for lifting the odd-numbered groups of warps and one for the even ones.

Twills, a class of textiles easily recognised by strong diagonal lines, also have threads that go over and under units of one or two warp threads, but as the point of intersection moves one place to the left (or right) on each successive row, the warps included in each have to be threaded up in such a way that they can be lifted up consecutively. In a twill in which the weft goes over-one-under-two, written 1/2, three lifting devices, or shafts, are used and the warps are threaded in succession 1,2,3 and repeated. In a 2/2 twill, four shafts are used and the warps threaded in succession 1,2,3,4 and repeated. Weaving a balanced twill on the latter example, the shafts are lifted in sequence in pairs, starting with 1 and 2, followed by 2 and 3, 3 and 4, and 4 and 1, each thread floating over two in both the warp and weft direction. If either the direction of threading or the order of lifting the shafts is reversed, the diagonal lines reverse direction; and if both regularly reverse in the same cloth, weave structures with familiar names such as herringbone and bird's eye result.

32 (above) *Basket weave, an extension of plain weave.*

33 (below) *A balanced twill that intersects over and under two threads at a time.*

34 *Indonesian* tampan. *This ceremonial ship cloth from Kroë, south Sumatra, is a fine example of supplementary weft. London, Victoria and Albert Museum.*

Many of the weave structures encountered in the countries described in this book are termed 'compound weaves' (Emery, 1980, p. 140), because they combine a simple ground weave (tabby) with an additional supplementary weft or warp as the decorative element in the textile.

Supplementary wefts are the easiest way to introduce decorative motifs into an otherwise plain cloth. The supplementary weft yarn, usually coloured, and also thicker than that used in the ground weave, floats over several warp ends at a time, a device which, if unsupported by a ground weave, leads to a loose, unstable fabric. The decorative weft is either used from selvedge to selvedge, or is introduced in isolated areas. The points at which the supplementary thread is tied down by the warp threads going over them are called binders, and the positioning of these sometimes produces secondary patterns.

A characteristic of elaborate scenes worked in supplementary weft, as in the *tampans* from Indonesia, is that the cloth has a positive and a negative face, one showing a dark design on a light ground, and the other a light design on a dark ground. This is easy to understand when it is realised that the supplementary weft, when not appearing on the face of the cloth, is floating on the reverse.

Supplementary warps are comparatively rare, the technique being far less 35 versatile. Not only do the additional decorative threads have to be planned in advance, so that they can be incorporated in the making of the warp, but they cause problems with the tensioning, since the supplementary warps are taken up at a different rate from the ground weave ones, as there are fewer intersections. Because of this, constant adjustments have to be made to the warp during weaving.

The additional weft threads in supplementary weft are not under tension, so the same problem does not arise. However, in complex supplementary weft patterning much preliminary work follows after the warp is mounted on the loom. Warp sticks are inserted under the warp threads to be lifted, row by row, for the whole repeat of the design, after which, in some cases, they are replaced by heddles. Details of this and other methods of inserting the supplementary weft are given in the relevant chapters.

35 *Decorative cloth from Sumba, Indonesia, woven in supplementary warp.*
London, Victoria and Albert Museum.

Other compound weaves include those that have two or more complementary sets of warps, or both warps and wefts as in the double and triple cloths, and those with warps that cross and recross each other as in the gauze weaves, but this chapter is limited to describing the structures that the reader will encounter in this book.

In this context there remains one more technique, twining, which is used in many textiles for starting and finishing borders, but for the entire textile in twined tapestry. Strictly speaking, twining is not a weaving technique, as we shall see, but as the construction is also of two sets of threads at right angles to each other, and the technique is often used in conjunction with a woven fabric, it is included here. In twining there is not one weft thread, but a pair or more of threads which twine around each other enclosing a warp thread (or group of threads) between each turn. Its likeness to basket making is obvious, and it is possible that twining was the first textile technique to evolve. A loom is needed – or if not a loom a bar for free-hanging warp threads – but no shedding device, as the twining takes place on a passive warp, and no shuttles as the wefts are put in with the fingers.

The use of twining as a starting and finishing border, sometimes consisting of only two rows with the opposite twist in each, is not only decorative but fulfils the important function of spacing the warp threads. The twist between the warps holds them firmly in position, the thickness of the two wefts determining the space between the warps.

Compact weft twining of a large area, for example in the twined tapestry textiles woven on the horizontal ground loom by the bedouin, can be confused with interlaced tapestry unless examined closely, when it will be noticed that each weft as it covers a warp lies at a slight angle due to the twist at each intersection. In plain weave tapestry, the weft showing between two warps lies at right angles to the warps.

In conclusion, the object of these preliminary chapters has been to provide a background to the three skills that go towards the making of a textile, spinning, dyeing and weaving, and the many choices that accompany them: choice of fibres

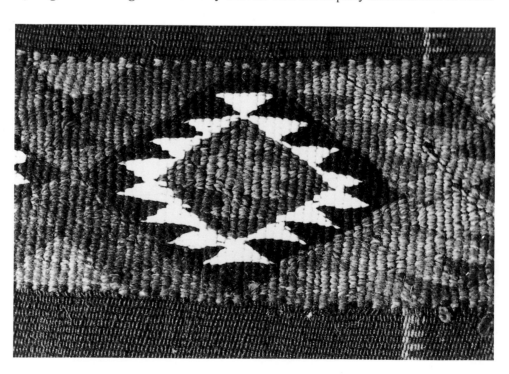

36 Twined pattern area on a warp-faced textile: part of a bedouin tent-dividing curtain. British Museum.

and how to spin them, of colours and how to obtain them, and of structures and how to execute them. Given this amount of choice it may seem surprising that the textiles within each chosen area have such a strong family likeness. For example, it is not likely that a supplementary weft or *ikat* from Indonesia would be mistaken for a brocade from Guatemala or a *kasuri* fabric from Japan. The techniques may be the same, but the results could not be more different.

What determines the choice? The power of tradition, based initially on availability of materials but constantly changing in response to new situations; children who learn from their elders and who pass on their skills. Parameters are set and the weaver creates from within the invisible framework, although still with considerable scope for individuality. This security might be envied in a so-called civilised country in the West where the textile traditions of cloth-making have been taken over by machines, making them no longer relevant to the hand-weaver.

But other challenges have come to fill the gap. Some weavers in the West work hand in hand with manufacturers designing textiles on the handloom for later production on high-speed machines; others use thread as a means of expression, elevating weaving to the status of fine art, the status now also accorded many of the textiles described in this book.

37 *Compact weft twining in the Wahiba sands, Oman.*

a

b

c

1 NORTH AMERICA

The Navaho

The Navaho inhabit the northern part of Arizona and New Mexico, bounded to the north by Utah and Colorado. The two big tributaries of the Colorado river, the Little Colorado and the San Juan, more or less define the northern and western boundaries of their territory. Shut in on all sides from the ocean by mountain regions and wide tracts of land, the area is without rain for large parts of the year.

This, then, is the setting for a tradition of weaving which is unique. Rugs are woven all over the world, but Navaho rugs are quite distinctive in both design and technique. The designs have evolved from simple beginnings in the eighteenth century, elaborating in response to constantly changing demands during the second half of the nineteenth century, and finally returning to a new-found simplicity today. During all this time the actual technique of weaving has remained virtually unaltered.

Before looking in detail at these rugs, it is essential to consider the background of the Navaho. The Spanish introduced sheep into the south-west in the second half of the sixteenth century and the Navaho, in their numerous incursions across the border, began to acquire large flocks. Looking after sheep suited their nomadic way of life and formed the basis of their economy, producing food, wool and clothing. In the second half of the nineteenth century they were recorded as owning over half a million sheep, although their own population did not exceed 10,000 (Dockstader, 1978).

At the outset, in the 1700s, the Navahos wove only for their own use: lightweight blankets worn around the shoulders, saddle throws and bedding. The blankets may have been modelled on the Mexican *serape*: Navaho women taken as slaves by the Mexicans were set to weaving, and when they returned to their homes may well have brought back the idea of a wide, simply striped, blanket-shaped shawl. Likewise, the Navaho men took Pueblo women for their wives, and they already had weaving skills which would have been assimilated by the other women. Also the Navaho who were tragically herded into the Basque Redondo in the 1860s were issued with Mexican blankets ordered in thousands by the United States army. All these influences were at work, but there was one fundamental difference between the Mexican and Navaho weaving: the Mexicans used cotton and the Navahos wool.

The so called 'classic period' of weaving from 1850 to 1875 begins with the four phases of the chief blankets, although these were not exclusively for chiefs as they were also traded with other Indian tribes. The four phases are useful categories reflecting the development of the design of the lightweight blankets worn around the shoulders, the width of which far exceeded the length.

The first phase comprises the simplest blankets, usually banded in black or a strong indigo dyed blue/black on a white ground. In the second phase the wide bands are broken by the introduction of small rectangular areas of colour within the broad stripes. The third phase not only introduces colour into the stripes, but the simple rectangles previously confined to areas within the broad bands now

38 *Chief blankets. The main features of the first three phases: (a) first phase; (b) second phase; (c) third phase.*

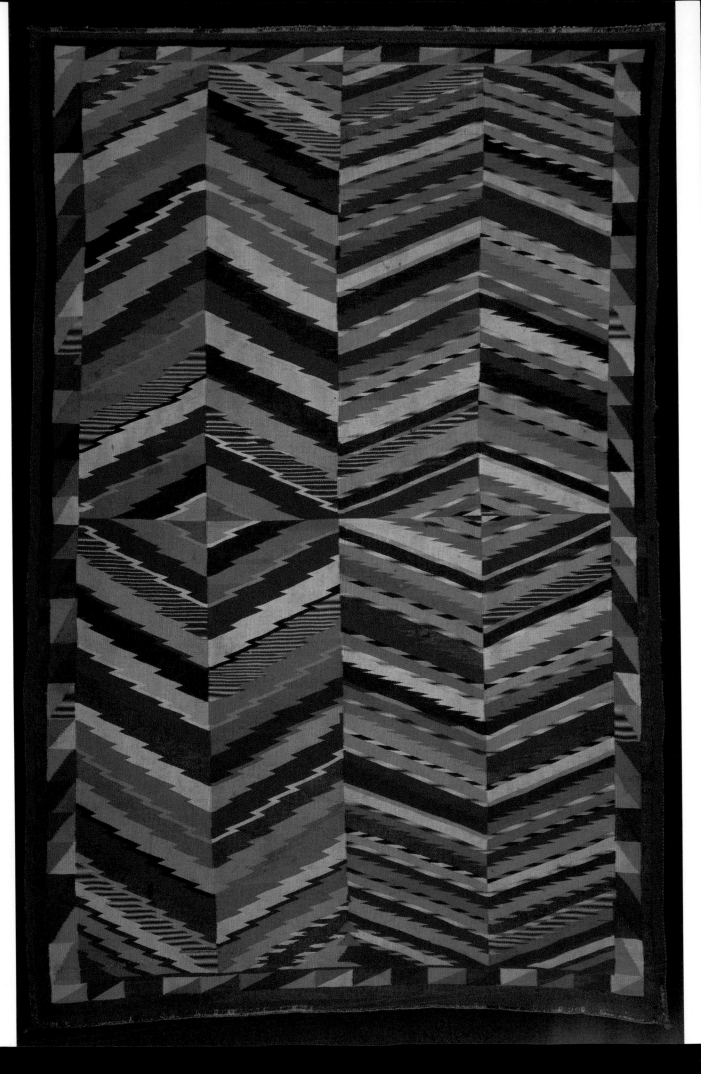

break out into the ground area in stepped diamonds. The fourth phase forms a link between the overall horizontal shape of the first three phases and the more conventional rug shape (with the warp running the length of the longest measurement rather than the shortest one) of all subsequent weaving. The diamonds which were tentatively escaping from the bands in the third phase have become the dominant feature, and in order to accommodate this new departure in design the overall dimensions have had to change.

Some wool dyed with natural colours was used in these early blankets, but the colours available to the Navahos from their natural environment did not produce the strong and vivid colours which are associated with the classic period of weaving. Indigo, imported by the Mexicans from Europe, and Mexican cochineal could both be bought from the Pueblos at a price, but, strangely enough, the most common source for coloured yarn was the bright red *bayeta*. *Bayeta* is the Spanish word for baize, a light-weight woollen cloth which in this case had been dyed red with cochineal before being imported by the Spanish in Mexico for making up into military uniforms. The Navahos bought this cloth, laboriously ravelled it, and then re-spun the fibres by hand to make the type of high-twist yarn they were used to.

During the last quarter of the nineteenth century, the railway was pushing its way from east to west and in its wake bringing white tourists into the interior. Traders were quick to see the potential in sales of native weaving to the tourists, and the Navaho, seeing their chance to make an improved living, were also accommodating in altering the shape of the blankets. They now started to produce vertical, rectangular-shaped blankets in vivid colours with dazzling design – the 'eye-dazzlers' as they are called – supplementing the *bayeta* red with 'Germantown' yarns, an American lustrous four-ply machine-spun yarn dyed in many colours.

Unhappily, this peak of achievement was not sustained in quality although it was to be surpassed in quantity. Many different circumstances were responsible for this lowering of standards. The size of the flocks, which were now larger than they had ever been, the new demand for rugs in addition to blankets, and the availability of cheap aniline dyes which were easy to use resulted in the Navahos finding it more economical to spin and dye their own fleece and to discontinue buying the *bayeta* cloth and Germantown yarns. This in itself was not a recipe for disaster, but when added to the enormous increase in demand for their weaving, the result was a lowering of standards. Coarser yarn was used; the coarser the yarn, the fewer rows per inch, and the fewer rows per inch the quicker a rug can be woven.

The result of this downhill spiral was the increased influence it gave to individual traders. They were now in a position either to insist on the highest quality, thereby being able, by charging a high price to the buyer, to pay the weaver a fair price; or simply to buy the rugs by weight regardless of quality and sell to the undiscriminating tourist. The result was, and in fact still is, interesting, because a situation arises unusual in other areas of rug weaving, where on the one hand there is a weaving élite, recognised 'names' whose rugs are sought after and which command high prices; and on the other, unrecognised weavers who barely get sufficient reward for the long hours, days and weeks it takes to spin, dye and weave a rug. It is now the older generation who are continuing the weaving tradition: the younger women are looking elsewhere for sources of income.

39 *Navaho 'eye-dazzler' blanket. British Museum.*

The loom

The Navaho loom comprises a stout upright frame erected in a convenient place either in or outside the home, within which the warp, previously prepared and already bound on poles, can be fixed. The two strong uprights of the frame may even be two trees which happen to be growing outside in the right position, but are more likely to be poles, even abandoned telegraph poles, specially selected for the purpose and sawn to the correct length. The two uprights having been securely fixed in the ground, with additional supports at an angle near the base if needed, top and bottom cross bars are lashed in position. This simple structure comprises the upright frame – the bare bones of the loom.

The method of warping and twining is worth studying in detail, as this is one of the keys to the unique character of Navaho rugs mentioned earlier. The warping frame also consists of two sets of parallel bars lashed together at right angles, only in this case the frame is horizontal. It lies just slightly above the ground, supported by large stones or small rocks. The two cross bars must be set apart from one another at a distance equivalent to the overall length of the rug, and should be long enough to accommodate its width.

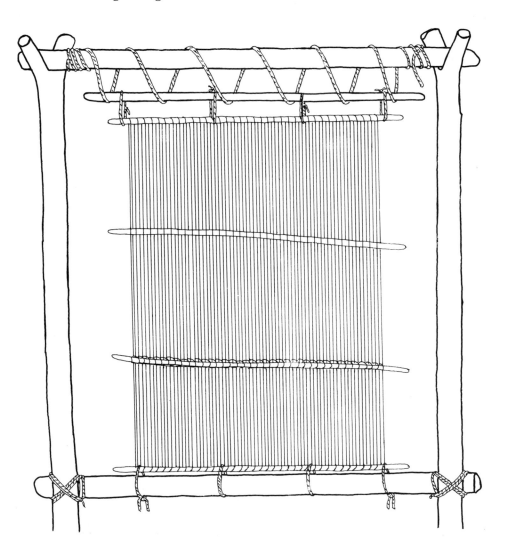

40 *Navaho loom. After an illustration in G. Reichard,* Navaho Shepherd and Weaver, *1936.*

The art of the loom

The warp, a hard-twisted woollen yarn wound into a convenient sized ball for handling, is attached to what will be the upper cross bar and taken down, under, and around the lower bar, up over and around the top bar, etc. in a 'figure-of-eight' formation, producing a cross in the middle. If the length to be warped is more than the stretch of one woman seated at the side midway between the two cross bars, then two women sit, one at each end, and roll the ball from one to the other. When sufficient warp has been wound for the width of the rug at about eight ends per inch (2.5 cm) it is tied off diagonally opposite the position from which it was started.

After securing the cross in the middle by tying two birch sticks, or other thin rods, on either side of the intersection, a long, fairly thick thread of the background colour of the rug is doubled over and twined along the width of the warp, both top and bottom, where the warp threads turn around the two poles. This twining thread serves the double purpose of evenly spacing the warp threads and making an edge which can later be lashed to new cross poles (or the same ones when dismantled from the warping frame), before the whole is transferred to the permanent weaving frame or loom.

When both ends have been twined, the two cross bars can be untied and carefully removed from the warp: care must be taken not to disturb the arrangement of the warp threads. The warp is then lashed to two poles, one at

41 *Navaho weaver: 'The blanket-maker' from* The North American Indian, *written and published by Edward Sherriff Curtis between 1907 and 1930.*

each end, with strong cotton twine or parcel string. In lashing, the string is passed *between* each pair of warp threads (that is *between* the loops), across the twined thread and round the pole, in order to make a very firm attachment of the warp to the poles; if it is a large rug, however, the string may be passed between every alternate pair of loops.

Finally, four or six separate strong loops are tied to the two poles at intervals ready to fix the warp in position in the upright loom. The bottom pole is attached directly to the lower cross bar of the loom, but the top pole is attached to an intermediary stout pole which in its turn is lashed with rope or wire to the top cross bar. When all is in position, the rope is tensioned by gathering up any slack right across from left to right and re-securing at the end. The success of this operation is vital to the success of the weaving of the rug.

This unique method of attaching the warp to the loom, perhaps born of the necessity to be economical in the use of yarn, leaves no warp ends at all. In hand-made rugs from the Middle East, or dhurries from India, there is always a fringe of warp ends at either end; or, if not a fringe, an alternative visible finishing of the warp ends which are left when a piece of weaving is cut from the loom. But when a Navaho rug is completed, it is dismantled from the loom as a finished article. Not an inch of yarn has been wasted or is surplus to requirements.

Yarns

When the Navaho first acquired their large flocks they spun their yarn from their own fleece. They have now taken this practice up again, but there was an intervening period when they bought their yarns. The commercial yarns available during the second half of the nineteenth century had the advantage of being dyed to a range of strong bright colours, giving a much wider choice than the natural colours available. The yarns were also ready for immediate use, which saved much time, as the following description of spinning will indicate.

Before the wool is spun the fleece has to be cleaned, but not washed, unless it is to be dyed. There are several reasons for cleaning rather than washing: in the first place, water is scarce; but, more importantly, the natural grease which is present in the fleece adds strength to the finished yarn, helps to repel dirt, and renders the finished blanket waterproof, as the grease also repels water. The fleece can be 'dry cleaned' by spreading it out in the sun and sprinkling it with powdered chalk or plaster of paris. When these powders are later shaken out, dirt shakes out with them. Afterwards the fibres of the fleece are teased apart, removing burrs and small pieces of vegetation which get caught up in the sheep's wool.

The fibres of the fleece then have to be carded. The carders are the only bit of equipment in the whole process of rug weaving that the Navahos have to buy rather than make or improvise for themselves. Carders, which are always used in pairs, are rectangular wooden boards approximately 9.5 × 12 in (24 × 30 cm), each attached to a handle on the longer side. The boards are covered with carding cloth, that is, a leather or canvas backing embedded with closely set wires, each one bent at an angle. The fleece, which is spread in small amounts on one carder, is brushed lightly with the other carder, disentangling and straightening the fibres and removing still more dirt. The fibres are transferred from one carder to another until they are all parallel and then they are removed ready for spinning.

A wooden spindle is used for this, with a shaft of about 18 in (45 cm) in length

42 *'Eye-dazzler' using Germantown yarns. This rug is unusual in that it has fringes.*
Bath, American Museum.

and a large flat spindle whorl near the lower end. The spinner sits on the ground with the shaft lightly resting against her right thigh at an angle of about 45°. Her right hand is used for rotating the spindle and her left hand for holding the prepared fibres and drawing them away from the upper end of the shaft, from which point the twist flips off and enters into the attenuated fibres. Only a little bit of twist is put in during the first spinning, producing a soft strand of loosely twisted wool the thickness of a middle finger. This is spun a second time, extending it in length and reducing its thickness, to produce the soft weft thread. For the warp yarn, which is continuously under tension on the loom, and which also has to withstand friction in the weaving, it is given a third and even fourth spinning, the additional twist adding greater strength. Plying two separate threads of singles yarn also gives strength to a thread, but the Navaho never do this except for the yarn they need for the binding threads on all four edges of the finished weaving.

Not all the fleece from the Navaho flocks is white: there are also 'black' and 'grey' fleeces, and these can be carded and spun separately to produce black and grey wool. However, there is room for much more subtlety if grey is produced by carding black and white wool together in varying amounts, according to whether a dark or light shade is required, and the two shades blended in the carding sequence, producing a whole new range of greys. These subtle shades of grey used together with natural dyed tans and yellows are characteristic of the rugs of the Two Grey Hills trading post. Pastel-coloured yarns can also be produced by mixing white and dyed fleece at the carding stage and can be found in the light backgrounds and flesh colours of the figures in the *yeis*, rugs depicting super-natural beings acting as intermediaries between the Navaho and their gods.

The commercial yarns available to the Navaho during the 'classic period' of weaving were the soft, lustrous three-ply Saxony yarns imported from Germany, and the Germantown yarns, an American four-ply wool named after the town in which it was manufactured. There was also, of course, the *bayeta* red already referred to at the beginning of this chapter and used in the production of the earlier rugs much sought after by collectors.

Dyes

The early blankets, woven before the introduction of aniline dyes, were limited in colour range, comprising: whites, browns, beiges, greys and black, all the product of naturally coloured fleece, some of which were blended while carding; dark blues dyed with indigo introduced by the Spanish in the seventeenth century; and red yarns ravelled from crimson *bayeta*. From the 1870s onwards, the colour range increased rapidly, either through the use of coloured commercial yarns or through dyeing the fleece or spun yarn with the new synthetic dyes. It was not until the 1920s and 1930s that a major change took place, misleadingly called a revival, utilising vegetable dyes in simple banded patterns. Approximately 150 colours are known to Navaho weavers today (Kent, 1985a, pp. 18–19).

The Navaho Indians use the plant material and minerals which are to be found in their surroundings. The vegetation ranges from lichen to cacti, for example the prickly pear growing in the desert; to wild cherry, oak, sumac and piñon, growing in the higher regions on the slopes of the mountains; and to smaller trees and bushes growing wherever water is to be found, by the side of small streams.

44

The yarn has to be thoroughly washed before dyeing, as the dye does not 'take' if there is dirt or grease present in the wool – it acts as a barrier. Nowadays soap is widely available for washing, but before this was so, the Navaho used two types of sword-leaved soap plant, both of the yucca genus, one growing on the lower slopes and the other at a higher altitude. The dried or fresh yucca root was crushed and rubbed between the hands in cold water until a lather was produced. Warm water was then added and the yarn immersed in it, after which it was thoroughly rinsed and hung out to dry.

The second prerequisite for successful dyeing is, in most cases, a mordant. Lichens are an exception, being substantive dyes. Alum, one of the most useful mineral salts used as a mordant, is found in its natural form in deposits, especially around the sulphur springs in New Mexico. It is a white crystalline substance and is found where there has been recent water evaporation. Sometimes the Navaho burn the alum before using it, but it can also be used just as it is. An alternative mordant used by the Navaho is water in which juniper ashes have been steeping. A branch of juniper is held over a pan while the green needles are set alight, the ashes being caught in the pan below (Bryan, 1978, p. 17).

In other parts of the world, where water is abundant or taken for granted, the wool is usually mordanted before dyeing as a separate process, but in the Navaho country where water is a precious commodity the mordant is added to the dye bath halfway through, the two processes, mordanting and dyeing, thus being accomplished in a single operation.

When the dye material consists of twigs, bark or roots, the material has to be broken up or stripped into small pieces and put into a pan of water and given a preliminary boiling of several hours. The liquid is then strained, the mordant added and dissolved, followed by the wetted-out yarn, and the whole brought up to the boil and simmered until the desired colour is obtained. It is then allowed to stand overnight and the following day the yarn is rinsed and hung out to dry.

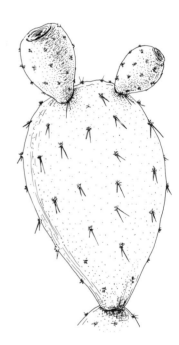

There are numerous recipes, many of which have been handed down from one generation to the next, but for the reader wanting to study them and follow up with practical experiments, a large number are collected together in *Navaho Native Dyes: Their Preparation and Use*, formulated by Nonabah G. Bryan, a Navaho, and compiled by Stella Young. Among them there is a very interesting description of how the fresh fruit of the prickly pear cactus is used to produce the pinks and deep roses so often found in Navaho rugs; in this case the fruit is not boiled in the way previously described, but fermented for one to two weeks according to the depth of colour which is required.

43 *The prickly pear* (Opuntia), *whose fruit is used for dyeing.*

Two other natural dyes used by the Navaho, not obtained from indigenous plants but bought from traders or from the Pueblo Indians, were indigo and cochineal, both of which are described elsewhere in these pages. However, as already pointed out, only a few natural dyes were in use before 1870 when the aniline dyes became readily available. These new dyes were cheap, easy to use, and came in a variety of colours. This explosion into colour came hand in hand with a change in direction in design, the simpler striped and rectangular designs or stepped diamonds being superseded by designs based on the diagonal, with aggressive zig-zaggy lines filling the ground area from corner to corner, as seen in the 'eye-dazzlers' of this period. The later rugs woven with naturally dyed yarns, on the other hand, reverted to the simpler formula of bands of colour, but with the addition of serrated patterns or stylised designs.

44 *Dye-plants growing in
Monument Valley, on the borders
of Utah and Arizona. In the left
foreground the yucca is in flower;
in the middle ground are low-lying
sage brush plants. The darker trees
behind are juniper.*

Now there is more flexibility in the choice of colour and design, many traditions are drawn on, and the same rug may contain yarns dyed with both vegetable and aniline dyes, for what is important is to obtain the desired quality of colour for each particular rug.

Weaving

The majority of the Navaho blankets and rugs are tapestry woven, although the Navaho are familiar with two-faced weaves, double-weave and twills.

Tapestry weave requires only two sheds, one of which is formed by the shed stick, which stays permanently in the loom underneath alternate warp threads. The other, the counter-shed, is formed by pulling on the heddle bar, which brings forward the warp threads not lifted by the shed stick (see Fig. 40). The two-faced weaves, the double-weave and the twills need four sheds and therefore require four heddle bars (or three heddle bars and a shed stick) and were not so often used.

Tapestry weave, in which the warp is covered and only the weft shows, requires an extremely strong and taut warp on which the softer weft yarn, put in carefully with just the right amount of slack, can 'bed down'. Two techniques are used to ensure that the weft covers the yarn and at the same time helps to avoid the tendency for the weaving to narrow as the work progresses: in one the weft is laid-in in scallops before being beaten down by the wooden comb across the

45 *Four Navaho rugs. Rug (a), with yellow, green, white and black serrated lozenge shapes on a red ground, dates from about 1900. Rugs (b), (c) and (d) combine carded mixtures of fawn and grey with black, white and red. See also Figs. 46 and 48.*
British Museum.

a

b

width of the web; and in the other the weft is held gently at an angle in the shed, the additional length producing enough slack if it is beaten down against the previous row starting from the point opposite to which it is being held, that is from the selvedge. Different sized wooden combs are used for beating.

The simplest form of design in a weft-faced weave is made up of horizontal stripes in contrasting colours. This was the first design element used by the Navaho and could serve as a model for someone embarking on their first rug in the Navaho technique. It leaves the weaver free to concentrate on the basic principles of the technique, with the weft travelling from selvedge to selvedge, before embarking on the diagonals and vertical colour changes of all the other developments in design. An additional feature which could also be mastered at this stage is the braiding that strengthens the selvedge, another of the unusual features of a Navaho rug. Just as the warp was braided at the top and bottom before being mounted on the loom, so the edges are braided as the weaving proceeds, the beginnings and ends of all four braids being tied together at the four corners when the rug is taken off the loom, producing the familiar short tassels.

46

c

d

47 (opposite, top) *Central motif of chief blanket (third phase), showing the dovetailing of two colours in the vertical colour changes, and 'lazy lines' in the white areas.*
British Museum.

48 (opposite, bottom) *Detail of the diamond motif in the rug illustrated in Fig. 45d, showing the serrated edges, some of which are outlined in a contrasting colour.*

To set up the braiding, a length of plied yarn is needed for each side (three times the length of the rug) and each is doubled over and attached to the lower beam on either side. The other ends are temporarily attached to the upper beam, the two strands being separated and one placed in front of the shed stick and the other behind. The end in front of the shed stick acts as the outer warp end for six or so rows, after which the two ends are reversed, the one from behind being brought forward in front of the shed stick and the one from the front being taken behind. As these two ends are always exchanged by twining in the same direction, braids are gradually woven into and up the sides. The twining of the two ends accumulates twist above as well as below, so the top ends have to be untied from time to time to allow the excess twist to escape.

Tapestry weave usually implies weaving in several colours, *not* travelling from selvedge to selvedge but only covering the predetermined area, and this is the technique used in the majority of Navaho rugs and blankets (apart from the first phase of the chief blankets). There are several methods of doing this. One is to lay the appropriate colour in the correct position, for example each colour starting from the right and working towards the left, and beaten in; the shed is then changed and, starting from left to right, each colour is taken back to the same, or a new, position as dictated by the design. In another method, particularly on a large rug, the weaver sits in front of one portion of the warp and weaves up a complete design element, a diamond for example, afterwards filling in the area around it. (The design element must be a shape that is reducing in size or else there would be nothing for the new row to be beaten against; if the shape increases in size, the background must be put in first and the shape filled in afterwards.) The weaver then changes her position and weaves another element in the same way. Even if she has a large area of the same colour to weave, she is likely to break it up with a diagonal line, partly in order to keep within an area of colour easy to reach but also to keep the weft tension consistent throughout, both on the design and plain areas. These lines produced in the plain areas of colour are known as 'lazy lines'. 47

46 *Detail of the rug illustrated in Fig. 45b, showing dovetailing of colours and braiding selvedge.*

49 *Techniques of tapestry weaving:*
(a) colour steps one to the right on each successive pass;
(b) steep triangular shapes made with a series of steps (expanded view, see also Fig. 50);
(c) the 'wedge' method;
(d) linked wefts.

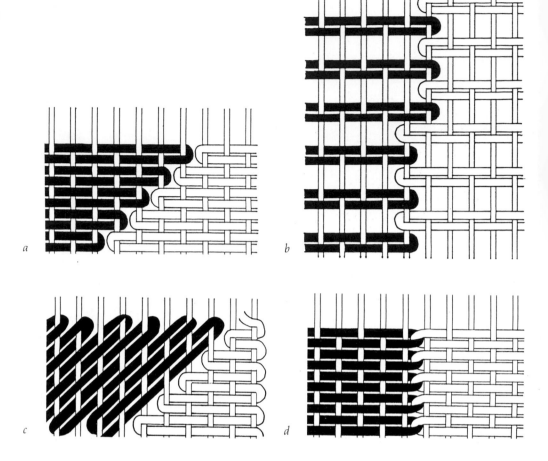

Diagonal lines producing serrated shapes, lightning effects or deep triangular areas of colour are the most frequent design elements in the classic period. Shallow triangular shapes are made by the colour travelling backwards and forwards, each time stopping short one warp thread before the last, either at one end or both according to the shape being produced. 48

Zig-zagging lines, or lightning effects, can be produced row by row, or by the 'wedge' method (which distorts the warp and is sometimes referred to as the 'distorted warp' method). In the wedge method one side of a triangle is woven on the edge of the design and all subsequent stripes are laid in at an angle against the sloping side of this triangle across the width of the weaving until they reach the other edge, when the same procedure is followed. 49

Steep triangular shapes have to be 'stepped'; that is, the overall angle of the shape has to be achieved by a series of dovetailed steps, the colour travelling backwards and forwards over the same warp threads for six or eight rows in each step. 50

Long vertical colour changes can also be treated in this way, although there are other ways of dealing with vertical colour changes (see diagrams). Long vertical colour changes appeared when the demand from tourists for floor rugs rather than blankets suggested designs contained within a border rather than covering the whole field. In fact some of the designs even began to resemble oriental rugs. 46

By no means all Navaho rugs are made up of abstract designs. Many are

50 *Detail of the blanket illustrated in Fig. 39, showing steep triangular shapes achieved by a series of steps.*

51 Yeibichai *figure, from a rug woven by Irene Williams. Shiprock area, New Mexico. London, Horniman Museum.*

pictorial, depicting objects of everyday life on a plain background – images of trains, trucks, the American flag, or even 'Snoopy'. Other twentieth-century subjects are designs depicting the *yeis*. Designs which until then had been carried out by medicine men with coloured sands on the ground and destroyed at the end of the ceremony, are now being woven as hangings and causing mixed feelings. 'Textiles designed as sandpaintings are not considered sacred by the Navaho, but their weaving is still subject to disapproval by conservative members of the tribe' (Kent, 1985a, p. 17). There are also *yeibichai* rugs which depict the Navaho dancers impersonating *yei* spirits.

Spirits play an important part in the Navaho world, even in the process of weaving: for example, spirits inhabit the sword and the comb used in beating down the weft, and there are certain taboos about what you may and may not do when handling these implements.

The women, who are the weavers, dovetail the various activities of spinning, dyeing, warping and weaving into their other activities of attending to the home and minding the flocks. They teach each other, and occasionally privileged outsiders, by a method of 'showing': no discussion takes place, no long verbal explanations, just a simple system of 'watch' and 'do'. Through allowing a few outsiders to live with them, their traditions have been passed on to people outside the Navaho reserves, and the results are there for us to learn from, as a glance at the titles in the bibliography at the end of this book will show.

The Navaho 57

2   THE MIDDLE EAST

The bedouin

The bedouin are the nomadic tribes of the Arabian peninsula, constantly on the move in search of pasture and water for their animals. Thousands of miles are travelled, from the Syrian desert in the north to Oman in the south-east, from the Jordanian desert in the west to the borders of Iraq in the east, even through the vast area of the Empty Quarter.

Conditions in the desert are extremely harsh. The average temperature by day is 86°F (30°C) but can soar as high as 120°F (49°C), while at night it falls to 40°F (4°C) or below. There is not much rain at any time of the year and grazing is hard to find. Storms blow up, whirling the sand around, covering everything and obscuring the tracks.

The bedouin's livelihood and source of wealth are his animals. Some people say that the 'true' bedouin is the one who keeps camels: these bedouin can range farther afield, as camels are capable of travelling long distances without food or water. The sheep-breeding bedouin keep nearer to the edges of the sands where pasture is more likely to be found, and have more contact with the settled communities.

52 *A bedouin tent in Oman, made from lengths of hand-woven material.*

The bedouin are Arabs and followers of the Islamic faith. 'The Arabs are the oldest race on earth; they date from the flood!!' Gertrude Bell is here quoting the opening lines of an essay on the customs of the Arabs written by her Arabic teacher (*Selected Letters of Gertrude Bell*) which she obviously took with a pinch of salt (hence the exclamation marks). Nevertheless, the bedouin are said to trace their descent back to the biblical patriarch Abraham, himself a nomad, and the Old Testament is so full of references to the nomadic way of life that studying the bedouin makes it far easier to visualise the scenes in the stories of the Bible.

Much has been written on the life of the bedouin by travellers of the nineteenth and twentieth century. From travelogues, diaries and letters a picture builds up of both their physical and spiritual toughness, the simplicity of their life with so few worldly goods that house and possessions can be packed up and moved in no time at all, their legendary hospitality even when food is scarce, and their reliance on each other, far from civilisation.

Of course one cannot say 'far from civilisation' any more, for with the discovery of oil, which brought in its wake the building of air strips and roads, such rapid changes have taken place that the life of the bedouin has changed too. Already television aerials have appeared above the tents, and trucks are parked where previously camels would have been couched: water is carried in truck inner-tubes rather than the traditional goats' skins.

Still persisting, however, is the bedouin home, a woven tent. Made to measure, it can vary in length from approximately 10 to 40 feet (3–12 m), the size of the tent reflecting the importance of the owner. The one described by Moses in Exodus was even larger, as the following description shows (a cubit equals the length of the forearm):

They made hangings of goats' hair, eleven in all, to form a tent over the Tabernacle; each hanging was thirty cubits long and four cubits wide, all eleven of the same size. They joined five of the hangings together, and similarly the other six. They made fifty loops on the edge of the outer hanging in the first set and fifty loops on the joining edge of the second set, and fifty bronze fasteners to join up the tent and make it a single whole (Exodus 36:14).

As this description indicates, a bedouin tent consists of a rectangular roof made from several strips of cloth sewn together. The cloth is warp-faced and woven from natural black hand-spun goat's hair. The black goat's hair has greater strength than wool, an important consideration in material for a tent, but if it is not available in sufficient quantity goat's hair may be used for the warp and wool for the weft. Narrow decorated strips are sewn across the large pieces to give added strength at the points where the guy ropes are connected. This rectangular roof is hoisted up on central posts (75 in or 190 cm in height) with smaller ones (55 in or 140 cm) each side. Wooden shoes or rags are lodged between the top of the posts and the fabric. The roof is erected with one long side backed to the wind, its flat shape presenting the minimum of resistance. A long piece comprising the sides is then attached to the roof, held in position by large wooden pins. Alternatively, the roof can hang down to the ground on each short side, in which case no side pieces are needed at each end but only a long one at the back. The walls, like the roof, are also made of several lengths of cloth joined together: the top and bottom pieces wear out before the centre, the top from the constant pinning and unpinning and the bottom from being buried in the sand to

53 *Warping: (right) adjusting the position of the warp thread before throwing the ball to the woman at the other end; (below) making the continuous heddle. Oman.*

54 *(a) the shed and (b) the counter-shed; (c) shows the sword being used on edge to increase the space.*

keep out draughts. As the strips wear out, they are replaced by adding new pieces in the centre so that the worn-out pieces on the edge can be discarded. With constant renewal of worn-out pieces, one tent lasts a family a lifetime.

Except in cold weather, the front of the tent is left open, but a long, often richly decorated length of cloth, the *saha*, divides the right-hand (or eastern) side of the tent for the use of the men and guests from the rest. This extends out further than the roof covering, but in cold weather can be folded round to enclose the open side. In a large tent a division is also made on the left-hand side to mark off a cooking area. The large central space contains all the family's belongings, the bedding, cushions and carrying bags, a child's hammock perhaps, the loom, and a canopy used by wealthier women when travelling.

The members of one extended family will pitch their tents close together; the long guy ropes cross each other and provide a network of ropes for the unwary to trip over but at the same time giving protection for the inhabitants (Faegre, 1979, p. 20). When water and food for the animals is scarce, however, each family will travel separately, pitching its tent apart from the others to increase the chance of finding enough pasture.

With their herds of camels, goats and sheep, the bedouin are almost self-sufficient. The animals provide meat and fat, milk for making cheese, and butter; wool and hair for the weaving of their tents, storage bags, cushions, rugs, ropes and reins; and the sale of an animal provides ready cash for buying coffee, rice, salt, dates and cooking utensils, or even a television set.

The ground loom

56 The horizontal fixed-heddle ground loom used by the bedouin is a very simple affair. The two stout beams needed to hold the warp under tension are positioned behind pegs driven into the ground and lashed to them. The heddle bar is supported on either side of the stretched-out warp by two rocks (or large cans, whatever is to hand) of similar size. The continuous heddle attached to the heddle bar lifts up every alternate thread, making a shed through which to pass the weft. The threads for the counter-shed pass over a thick, flat rod behind the fixed heddle. If this rod is brought nearer to the fixed heddle and is turned up on edge it
54 forces this second lot of threads above the height of the first, thereby producing the counter-shed. A few more sticks — one a carefully fashioned sword stick,
55 others for picking up pattern rows, yet more stick shuttles for the weft — and a metal hook or gazelle horn for helping to force the weft in position, complete the equipment.

To weavers in the West, with their four-, eight- or sixteen-shaft looms, it seems hardly believable that textiles so rich in design, and some so complex in structure, are woven on such simple looms. The weaving is the work of women, and is just one of the many household tasks which they perform.

The distance between the two beams and the width of the warp is determined by the length of the finished weaving. Allowance must be made for the take-up of the warp, which is quite considerable in warp-faced weaving. The warping is
53 done *in situ*. Two women sit, one at each end, facing each other, and a child with a ball of warp yarn runs between the two. The warp is not usually wound directly on to the two beams, so each woman holds a stout rod in one hand over which to pass a loop of the yarn. The rod is lashed to the beam every ten to twelve warp

55 *Detail of the loom in Fig. 56, showing the sword used in opening the shed; also the stick spool and heddle bar.*

56 *A horizontal ground loom in Israel. The heddle bar is supported on either side by rocks.*

threads, the cord being held firm in the meantime with the toe (Grace Crowfoot, *The Tent Beautiful*).

Grace Crowfoot also mentions that the warp is wound directly on the rods without making a 'figure-of-eight' in the usual manner, but looping the continuous heddle around alternate threads as the warping progresses. Violetta Thurstan, on the other hand, writes, 'The weaver, sitting on the ground, makes the cross of the shed as she goes, before winding it on the stick which serves as a cloth beam' (*A Short History of Decorative Textiles and Tapestries*, 1934, p. 92). It is probable that both methods are used: the advantage of forming a figure-of-eight when warping is that it maintains the order of the threads and reduces them to one level at the point of crossing. If the warp is wound from one bar at one end of the loom to the other at the other end with no crossing in the middle, the result is two layers of threads (owing to the thickness of the bar) and problems identifying the correct sequence.

If the continuous heddle is not put in at the time of warping it can be put in afterwards in order permanently to lift up one set of alternate threads; those threads not lifted by the heddle bar, pass over the shed stick lying behind it. The diagram shows the space through which the weft is passed in both the shed and counter-shed. It looks simple, but in fact, because of the density of the warp threads in a warp-faced fabric, and the tendency of wool and hair to cling to itself, the two sheds are extremely difficult to make and require a great deal of physical effort. It is no exaggeration to say that the weaver has to struggle for each row, forcing the threads handful by handful up or down according to the shed she needs.

When the weaving has progressed to a point where it is difficult to reach the warp threads and make the shed, instead of rolling up the part already woven on the cloth beam the weaver simply changes her position, moving up closer to the part she wants to reach and sitting on the part she has just woven. At the same time she must move the fixed heddle and its supports further along the warp. So she continues along the length of the warp until the other end is reached, moving her own position and that of the heddle and its supports as she goes along. If before the weaving is completed it is necessary to strike camp, the whole thing, from one beam to the other, is wound up and loaded on to the camel (except for the rocks of course!). The bedouin loom shows remarkable similarities to the one

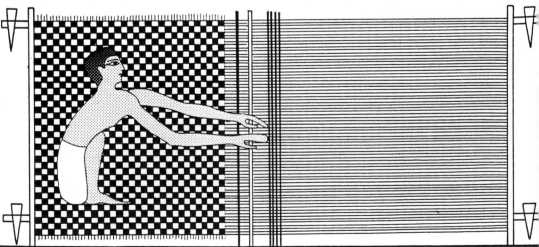

57 *A ground loom depicted in the tomb of Khety, no. 17 at Beni Hasan, Egypt. Middle Kingdom, 11th Dynasty, c.2020 BC.*

depicted in the Egyptian tomb of Khety at Beni Hasan (*c.* 2020 BC), although the strong check design and the projections from both selvedges suggest the weaving of a reed mat rather than a fabric. H. Ling Roth, in *Ancient Egyptian and Greek Looms*, analyses in considerable detail six different interpretations of a painting of a horizontal ground loom in the tomb of Khnumhotpe at Beni Hasan (*c.* 1900 BC). Among other things, he discusses the question, already referred to in this chapter, as to whether the warp threads were warped directly around the two beams, or on two narrower rods lashed to them. He also describes the Egyptian upright loom of this period, which is the loom still used by the settled people of the Middle East. But this loom, together with the pit loom, are not those used by the nomadic bedouin, and are therefore not discussed here.

Spinning

The fibres used by the bedouin in their weaving are goat's hair, camel and sheep's wool, and cotton. The hair and wool are from their own animals, but the cotton is imported and bought in the markets.

The sheep are sheared with scissors or hand shears (a type in use since Roman times) and the goat's hair is cut with a knife in a downward movement, but the wool and hair from the camel is plucked or combed from the animal at the time of moulting towards the end of the summer, or is picked up off the ground by a follower at the rear of the caravan trail.

The yarns are usually hand-spun by women and children using a spindle, an occupation which can be done at any time, especially when tending flocks or travelling. Occasionally men are seen twisting camel's wool by hand and winding it on to a stick for the weaving of udder bags.

The hair and wool fibres are neither combed nor carded, but teased out into a roving, a soft length of parallel fibres slightly twisted in the direction in which they are to be spun. This can be coiled up and put on the left wrist like a bracelet, or left as it is and thrown over the left shoulder out of the way ready for spinning.

In some parts of Oman, after the fibres are opened out to allow the removal of dust and chaff, the lock is streched out sideways across the knees and formed into a soft roll. This is extended and wound up in such a way that it can be held by a protruding loop on one finger. In many parts of the world the prepared fibres are attached to a distaff, but this is not part of the bedouin equipment. The reason for keeping the fibre safely out of the way, even if it is only in a neat pile with a stone on top, is to stop it from tangling with the thread being spun.

The spindles vary in size and detail, some having the whorl on top and others at the bottom, and the shaft varies in length from 14 to 19 in (36 to 48 cm). On the whole the spindle used by the bedouin has the whorl positioned at the top of the shaft, and it is made of a single bar or a crossed bar, above which is a hook.

The shaft is rotated either between the hands or along the thigh if kneeling or sitting down; or, if standing, by twirling between finger and thumb, or by a quick movement up the thigh before dropping it to rotate freely, referred to as the drop-and-spin method. If the spindle is rolled from the knee to the thigh, it sets the spindle rotating in a clockwise direction, which produces a 'z'-spun yarn.

The yarn to be dyed is made up into skeins; the rest is rolled up into balls. The yarn is plied in the opposite direction from the singles thread, either from two separate balls of yarn or from one big ball made up of two threads wound

66   *The art of the loom*

together. The same spindle can be used for plying, but a larger one holds more, thus accommodating the increased bulk. An interesting description of plying appears in a report written by Gigi Crocker in 1982 on weaving in Oman:

She plied on her right leg, in the usual manner, from a ball of two strands (combined) of singles. The yarn is overplied and completely twists back on itself when the tension is released. For approximately seventy centimetres of yarn (the length plied before winding on to the spindle again) she twisted the spindle shaft on her thigh an average of twenty-one times! But the yarn is always wound from the spindle into a firm, tight ball. This, in effect, sets or stabilises the yarn.

Yarn may not always be twisted to this extent, for there are as many different ways to spin and ply as there are spinners. For detailed descriptions of regional and geographical differences, the reader should refer to the writings of Grace Crowfoot, Shelagh Weir and Gigi Crocker.

Dyes

A riot of reds and oranges, with touches of blue, supplements the blacks, browns, beiges and white of the bedouin undyed handspun yarns. In former times these colours would have been dyed with natural dyes, but now it is far more likely that chemical dyes would be used. Even though the natural substances used in dyeing can still be found, either growing locally or on sale in the markets, chemical dyes are much quicker and easier to use.

As early as 1932 Grace Crowfoot and Louise Baldensperger, in their book *From Cedar to Hyssop: A Study in the Folklore of Plants in Palestine*, bemoaned the 'violent anilines' used by the dyers to satisfy their bedouin clients; but synthesised dyes based on the molecular structure of the original dyestuffs have taken the place of some of these. In their study they include recipes described to them for dyeing with madder and indigo to produce the reds and blues. Many of the other plants they found growing in Palestine are known to contain colouring matter, but how many of them were used for this purpose by the bedouin or the professional dyers of the towns and villages to whom they took their yarns, they do not say. The leaves of the almond tree for yellow and pomegranate bark for black are specifically mentioned; but other plants they found — alkanet, broom, safflower, camomile, elder, knotweed, sumac and henna — are all familiar plants to craftsmen of today interested in using natural dyes, and some of them were almost certainly used in the past.

The natural materials used for the reds and oranges would have been either madder, the roots of which are dried and crushed to form a powder, or kermes, a colour obtained from the dried bodies of an insect living on the kermes oak, a native of the eastern Mediterranean coast. Kermes is one of the most ancient dyes, the scarlet of the Bible, and was exported to the West in the Middle Ages. The colouring matter is produced in the female insects, which are collected and dried just before the eggs are due to be laid.

The madder roots contain the colouring matter alizarin, which was synthesised in the late nineteenth century: it is therefore possible to obtain the same colour with either the natural or the chemical dyestuffs. To quote from the pages of the same report on weaving in Oman mentioned earlier:

58 *Detail of a cushion cover from north-west Jordan in twined technique. The red from madder, blue from indigo and natural black and white yarns are typical of bedouin textiles. British Museum.*

Madder is still used in its natural form, though increasingly it is being replaced by a chemical powder that has the same name and can also be bought in the markets, though somewhat more easily. Natural madder is a root plant that grows in the Middle East, east India and now Europe. These roots, preferably three years old or more, must be pounded to a fine powder and mixed with the liquid from simmered, two year old, dried limes, the wool having first been mordanted in alum. To obtain a strong colour, the yarn should be dipped and dried three times. This procedure, including the mordanting takes anything up to one week. Whereas colour from a chemical dye could be obtained in a few hours (Crocker, 1982).

Indigofera tinctoria and other plants of the same genus, the natural source of the blue colouring matter indigo, are still being grown in some parts of the Arabian peninsula, but indigo has also been synthesised and the blue dye is readily available in powder form.

Jenny Balfour-Paul's account of fieldwork undertaken in the indigo-growing areas of South Yemen and Oman, and her description of dyeing, make interesting reading (1986, 1998). The recent work carried out by her and Gigi Crocker in the field has been valuable in recording, just in time, skills that may be in danger of disappearing altogether.

Weaving

The ground loom is used by women for weaving the tent, storage sacks, saddle bags, cushions and rugs, in fact a substantial part of the basic necessities of bedouin nomadic life. It is not used for fine materials for clothing; these are woven by men on the pit looms in the villages.

The articles woven on the ground loom range in scope from the simplest plain black material for the roof of the tent and the warp-patterned *saha* weave of the tent dividing curtain, to the complex one-weft double-cloth structure of camel girths. In addition there are the rich, colourful twined weaves used in the making of cushions, carpets and camel bags.

The rectangular roof of the tent, made up of several lengths sewn together, is woven from black goats' hair in plain warp-faced weave. For the sides of the tent, which are also made up of several strips, the weavers introduce other natural colours, either by sewing different lengths next to each other or by weaving wide and narrow stripes, spots and checks into the lengths. There are many variations in the way two contrasting colours can be used on a simple warp-faced weave, but they have to be planned in advance as they are the result of the colour sequence made at the time of warping. A broad stripe of brown sandwiched between two stripes of white, for instance, is made quite simply by warping the required widths of white, brown and white in that order. The change from one colour to another is often made by more subtle means, warping about 1 in (2.5 cm) of the area between each colour-change in alternate colours, one white, one brown, etc., which produces short horizontal lines of the two colours lying side by side, giving a 'dovetailed' effect. Different variations are achieved by other arrangements of colour in the warp, some of which are shown in the diagrams. 60 (The horizontal lines represent the shed and the counter-shed, and the symbols represent the different colours.)

These simple warp-faced stripes are sometimes completely covered over by 62 areas of weft twining. At first glance these areas of rich geometrical pattern, 63

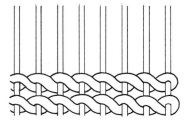

59 *Twining.*

68   *The art of the loom*

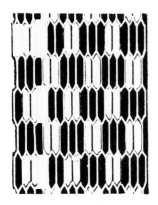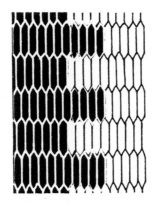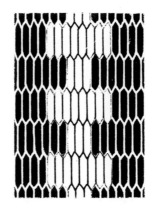

60 Three different colour
arrangements in warp-faced
fabrics, and, below, diagrams
showing the sequence for threading
each.

○ white
■ black
◕ white and red
warped together

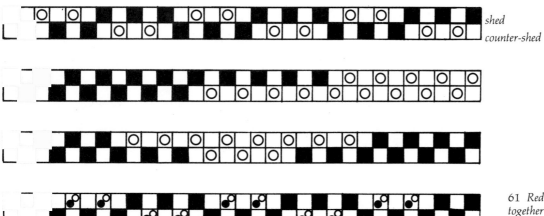

shed
counter-shed

61 Red and white warped
together for the 'pyramid' motifs of
the saha weave (see Fig. 64).

62 Detail of a warp-faced textile
with a corner of weft-faced
twining.
British Museum.

mostly based on triangles, look like tapestry weave similar to that described in the chapter on the Navaho. In fact, it is not weaving but twining, a technique which predates weaving in some parts of the world. Two weft threads spiral round each other, enclosing a warp thread (or in this case several warp threads) at each half twist, rather as in basket making. The twining is done on a closed shed, which may well be the reason for its use on the ground loom; the difficulties that are involved in changing the shed have already been mentioned in the description of the loom. Imagine two or three days spent weaving plain weave, actively struggling with the warp; thinking 'enough is enough' and changing to the slower, but less strenuous art of twining on the passive warp threads: but this is pure fantasy and one must stick to facts!

Weft twining produces a weft-faced surface, and for the thickness of hand-spun yarn used the warp is spaced about ten to twelve ends per inch (2.5 cm), allowing the weft to beat down and completely cover the warp. However, as twining is more often used in conjunction with warp-faced weaving, the twined areas have to envelop several warps at a time to avoid distorting the set of the cloth.

63 *Detail of a saddle bag, with simple warp-faced patterns covered by an area of weft-faced twining. British Museum.*

The twining may be done row by row always in the same direction, or in alternating directions to produce a chevron effect. The pair of twined threads put in at the start and end of a border or a rug are often done in two colours and opposing twists, adding a beaded look to the chevron effect.

65 The weavers' best efforts are reserved, however, for the *saha*, the curtain dividing the man and his guests from the family's quarters. The weave is so special to this dividing curtain that it has given its name to the technique which is referred to as *saha* weave, although the same technique is also found in other bedouin weaving.

66 In the dividing curtain, the *saha* weave is used for a long decorative panel in black and white running the length of the warp. Goat's hair is used for the black and cotton for the white. Sometimes the panel is contained between two narrow 64 borders of red and white pyramids, in various arrangements, with a granular effect, as each pair of red or white warps used in the pyramids is surrounded by black. At other times, these red, white and black pyramid designs are quite separate from the decorative panel, but run the length of the warp in the same piece.

64 *Detail of a storage bag, showing the characteristic pyramid design outlined in red, and the insertion of heavy tassels. British Museum.*

65 Part of a tent-dividing curtain made up of two panels of saha weave, two lengths decorated with twining, and a border strip (five lengths in all) sewn together. British Museum.

66 Two details from the saha pattern area of the curtain.

The bedouin   73

67 *Detail of a carpet made using the* saha *technique. British Museum.*

68 (facing page) *The discarded threads on the reverse of the carpet in Fig. 67.*

The art of the loom

The arrangement of colours in the warp for this narrow border can be seen in the diagram (Fig. 61). The red and white are warped together with black on either side. The pairs of red and white alternate with black between the shed row and the counter-shed row. It is this colour arrangement in the warp which gives the granular effect in the border. As each shed is made, the weaver has a choice of selecting either the red or the white warp thread on her pick-up stick, together with the raised black threads, and discarding the coloured threads not needed, which float behind.

The black and white threads for the decorative panel are also warped together. Here, though, the weaver has much more freedom in her choice of design and can give full expression to her individuality. Although there are many stylised designs which keep reappearing, with names such as 'pigeons' wings', 'camel trappings', or 'moon and stars', handed down from mother to daughter, there is no obligation to keep to them and therefore there is plenty of room to experiment. Each motif is enclosed in a rectangle or separated from the next by a small border across the band. The design of each motif is executed in the same manner as the pyramid borders: as each shed is made ready for the insertion of the weft, the weaver selects, out of each pair of threads which have been warped together, either a white thread for the background or a black thread for the motif, inserting the sword before passing the weft through. Many of the designs are based on diagonal lines, for the selection of the threads is made easier on each successive row if the black warp threads to be picked up are lying immediately to the left or the right of the one selected in the previous row.

69 Selecting the warp threads in the saha *pattern area.*

70 Camel saddle bag, showing the
elaborate finish at one end. Weft
twining covers warp-faced stripes,
and extra warp has been inserted
for the finger-woven tassels.
British Museum.

71 (facing page) *Detail of the saddle bag in Fig. 70.*

72 *Tassels from the saddle bag in Fig. 70.*

There is an ingenious development of this weave in which the floating warp threads on the back are also woven in, described in detail by Peter Collingwood in *The Techniques of Rug Weaving* (p. 450) and Martha Stanley in *In Celebration of the Curious Mind* (pp. 69–79).

No description of bedouin weaving would be complete without drawing attention to the splendid and multifarious methods used in the finishing of any one piece. Warp ends are woven into narrow strips, braided or bound and tassels attached. Sometimes large quantities of additional braids and pom-poms are added to camel bags and trappings, and as much care is lavished on a pair of camel's knee decorations as on rugs and cushions for the home. It is as though the richness of texture and colour compensates for the simplicity and hardships of the bedouins' life-style.

3　WEST AFRICA
Narrow-strip weaving

The countries of West Africa where there is a tradition of weaving cloth in narrow strips lie south of the Sahara, bounded by the Atlantic coastline to the west and south, and as far inland to the east as Lake Chad. The north of this area, on the fringes of the Sahara, is semi-desert, but the interior and coastline include tropical rain forests and areas of cultivation.

No one knows for sure why in this area, alone in the world, a tradition evolved for weaving strips of cloth much narrower than elsewhere, sometimes only 1 in (2.5 cm) wide but more usually 4 to 6 in (10 to 15 cm) in width. It has been suggested that a narrow web only requires a narrow lightweight loom and that this would have suited the early itinerant weavers travelling from one village to another.

Until recently the early history of the weaving of these narrow strips was gained from the observations of European travellers from the sixteenth century onwards; but during the 1960s Professor Huizinga of Utrecht in Holland recovered several hundred textiles while excavating the Tellem caves, located in the cliffs of the Bandiagara escarpment in the upper Niger delta. These textiles were also woven in narrow strips, using similar techniques to those of today, and the carbon dating of the bones of the skeletons in the burial chambers of these caves shows that the textiles date from the eleventh century. Until this exciting discovery it was not realised how far back in time the tradition of narrow-strip weaving extended.

73　*Trousers made from many different strips sewn together. Yoruba, Nigeria. British Museum.*

The narrow strips are made up into large cloths for everyday or ceremonial
73 wear, or into shirts, trousers, smocks and caps by sewing the strips selvedge to
selvedge: wider woollen strips of 14 to 16 in (35 to 40 cm) are sewn together for
blankets. In pre-colonial West Africa, these long strips of narrow cloth had
another value quite apart from their obvious use as textiles: the plain undyed
cloth, of more or less standard widths and lengths, was used as currency in
payment for goods or services. The recipient did not take it for making up into
clothing (as might be the case in a system of barter) but kept it stored away, as
money in the bank, so to speak, or passed it on again in payment for other goods.
The strip would be wound up, looking not unlike a coiled hose-pipe, or folded
zigzag fashion and tied into a bundle. Either way, the further the cloth travelled
from its place of origin, the more valuable it became. Trade worked its way north
from the coastal ports to markets such as Timbuktu on the edge of the sands (the
lucrative commodity on the return journey being salt), and extensive east-west
trade took place in the savannah belt between the Sahara desert in the north and
the forests of the south (Marion Johnson, *Cloth as Money: The Cloth Strip
Currencies*).

74 *Boy making the warp for a
man's loom. He carries the spools
of cotton on a bobbin carrier and
passes the threads round the pegs
in the ground. Nigeria.*

However fascinating it may be to consider this unusual use for narrow-strip weaving, its real interest for weavers lies not in the plain undecorated lengths, but in the wealth of patterned strips made for everyday wear and ceremonial occasions, bought in the markets or woven to order and then made up into finished cloths or garments by the local tailor.

There are pronounced differences in the appearance of the weaving from the various countries that make up West Africa. In the savannah belt of Mali and Upper Volta, where sheep are reared, the textiles are woven of wool, wider than the average, and made up into blankets. In Nigeria a small amount of non-lustrous hand-spun silk is sold in the local markets; it is produced from the cocoons of *Anaphe*, a species of wild moth, and this is often woven in its natural colour although it dyes well. By far the most frequently used fibre, though, is cotton: in former times it would have been grown and spun locally, but now is more likely to be machine-spun yarn. Two areas of West Africa where the weaving reached a peak of sophistication in the nineteenth century, and which are still important centres of weaving today, are Asante and Ewe in present-day Ghana.

The Asante kingdom grew rich and powerful from its deposits of gold, and by the nineteenth century had a well-developed form of government headed by the Asantehene and surrounded by his chiefs. In order to keep the court in the capital, Kumasi, supplied with luxurious silk cloths for ceremonial purposes, a skilled community of weavers was established at Bonwire, a village a few miles away. Here, master weavers and apprentices produced some of the most elaborate weft float designs to come out of West Africa. Although in former times the Asante produced simple striped designs in indigo on a white ground, they are now exclusively connected in people's minds with the production of Kente cloth, the complex weft patterning in blocks covering the width and length of the cloth.

These patterns required extra pairs of heddles and were often worked in silk, although silk and cotton were sometimes combined, silk being used for the weft and cotton for the warp. The silk used was not local wild silk as in Nigeria and other parts, but lustrous reeled silk imported in the form of cloth and ravelled for their own use – an interesting parallel with the Navaho who also imported cloth for ravelling (see Chapter 1). Shiny synthetic rayon is now a substitute for silk, and although the weaving speciality persists in Asante, some of the skills of the more elaborate designs have been lost.

The Ewe weaving in the Volta region has quite distinctive features, though the classification of textiles from this area is considerably confused by the fact that they also copied the famous Kente cloths. The designs which are characteristic of Ewe, and not likely to be confused with those of other countries, are in a representational, as opposed to abstract, style depicting animals, insects and objects or events of everyday life. Woven in weft inlay on a plain background, sometimes as many as seventy different motifs appear in one cloth, all 'travelling' in the direction of the warp.

Many of the West African textiles in our museums were acquired by traders in the nineteenth and early twentieth centuries; but more recently a large private collection was amassed by Alastair and Venice Lamb. Venice Lamb in particular has researched extensively into West African narrow-strip weaving, and the reader wanting to study the subject in depth is referred to the list of further reading at the end of this book.

The loom

Both men and women weave in West Africa. Until recently they wove on different looms: women wove on a vertical loom producing cloth for the family as an extension of their domestic duties; men wove on narrow, light, horizontal treadle looms as a profession. Now, however, the women's vertical loom is rarely seen, but many women have embraced the narrow treadle loom and work like men professionally producing narrow-strip cloth for sale.

At its simplest, the loom may be no more than a pair of shafts with pedals attached and a beater containing the reed, suspended from the branch of a tree, with two forked sticks supporting a narrow cloth beam in front of the weaver completing the equipment. Generally, though, some form of framework, either rectangular or in tripod form, is used to support the moving parts of the loom. A frame can be improvised from four uprights sunk into the ground and cross beams, all lashed together using any available branches which may be to hand. The Asante and Ewe, however, employ carpenters to make their looms. Within the framework the cloth beam is set at a convenient height for the weaver when sitting down; the pair of shafts, attached by cords, run over a smooth bar or a pulley suspended from the middle cross bar so that they can be raised and lowered by foot pedals. Cords, fastened at the end to a stick or piece of dried calabash, hang from the bottom of the two shafts, and are depressed alternately

76 *A pair of shafts attached to each other by cords running over a pulley above, and to foot pedals below.*

by the weaver raising and lowering the shafts, the cord running between his toes. The beater, a stout frame containing the reed, is also suspended from the framework. The bottom member of the beater frame is frequently made of a much heavier piece than the rest, the added weight contributing to the momentum when the beater is swung backwards and forwards. The pulley which holds the bobbin, over which the cord connecting the two shafts runs, may be elaborately carved in the form of human figures or animals, although the bobbin itself may only be a cotton reel. There are many regional differences in the pulleys, beaters and other parts of the loom, too numerous to describe here.

The most distinctive feature of the loom used in West African narrow-strip weaving is the absence of a warp roller. Instead of the warp being wound on the roller in the usual manner, it simply passes over a beam at the back of the loom and is stretched out 33 to 50 feet (10–15 m) in front of the weaver, the warp wound tightly round a stick and secured on a weighted sledge, tin tray or drinks crate. The weight is adjusted to give sufficient tension to the warp; and as the woven cloth is wound on to the cloth beam, the weighted warp is dragged towards the loom. As many as a hundred warps may be seen stretching out into a courtyard from one weaving shed, the weavers themselves remaining invisible as they sit in the shade.

78 *Long warps attached to dragweights. The Yoruba weavers are working in the shade. Nigeria.*

78

The art of the loom

The tripod loom is to be found particularly in Sierra Leone. As its name suggests, the structure for supporting the counter-balanced shafts is a tripod made by lashing three sticks or posts together. Unlike the box-frame type of loom, this one has no cloth or back beam; the warp is stretched out between two posts and the weaver sits *beside* the warp, operating the beater with a handle which projects out to one side from the top of the beater frame. Because the weaver is not sitting in front of a cloth beam on which he can wind the woven web, the tripod on which the shafts are suspended and the beater (which is floating, so to speak) have to be moved along the length of the warp as the weaving proceeds: this is similar in principle to the moving of the fixed heddle arrangement along the length of the warp of the horizontal ground loom already described in the chapter on bedouin weaving.

For the sake of clarity, the narrow looms so far described have referred to only one pair of shafts because this is all that is needed for the plain weave which accounts for much of the narrow-strip cloth. The Kente cloths, however, need two pairs of shafts, and the Asasia cloths (the royal cloths of Asante) required three pairs to produce patterns in twill. When there are two pairs of shafts, the back pair (the pair farthest from the weaver) carrying the *asanan* heddles are the first to be threaded, four to six ends being put in each heddle alternately. These heddles can be made of coarser yarn, as not so many are needed on each shaft; they are the pair used in the pattern areas of the cloth. The front pair, carrying the *asatia* heddles, are used for the ground weave, the individual warps being threaded up alternately; finer yarn is needed in the making of these heddles.

The heddles are made on a special frame and consist of two linked loops, referred to as 'clasped' heddles; this form of heddle allows for more play in use than the more usual 'eyed' or 'mailed' heddles.

This feature, and the narrowness of the loom, as well as the use of a dragweight in place of a warp beam, constitute some of the unique features of the West African narrow-strip loom.

Yarns

The yarns used in West African narrow-strip weaving include wool, goat and camel hair, ravelled thrown silk and wild spun silk, rayon and cotton. The bulk of narrow-strip weaving is in cotton, the cotton plant being well suited to the subtropical conditions.

There are, however, exceptions. On the southern edge of the Sahara the semi-nomadic peoples have small flocks of sheep, goats and camels, and fibres from their coats are spun to make yarn for blankets, sometimes using the wool as weft on a cotton warp. In Nigeria there is a tradition of collecting the cocoons of the *Anaphe panda* moth from the forest and selling them in the market for the wild silk they produce. The cocoons have to be broken into to remove the larvae (which if still alive are roasted and eaten) and are degummed by simmering in wood ash water (Picton and Mack, 1979, p. 28). The broken silk fibres are spun in a similar fashion to wool, not reeled straight from the cocoons as with cultivated silk. The result is a soft matt yarn, greyish-brown in colour, woven into a cloth called *sanyan*. Because of the expense of producing this material and its popularity with Yoruba men, a cotton imitation of it is now produced, also known as *sanyan*.

The lustrous silk used in the Asante cloths was not indigenous, but was ravelled silk yarn taken from material brought into the country as gifts or items of trade by the early explorers, or later imported during the period of colonisation. 'The red taffetas (11 yds in each piece) are unravelled by the Ashantees and wove into the cloths of their own manufacture' (Bowdich, 1819, p. 331). Synthetic rayon has now largely taken the place of silk for luxury cloths.

Cotton is still an important crop. Throughout Nigeria there are large textile mills machine-spinning and weaving. Traditionally the cotton was grown, harvested and spun by hand by women of all ages; it is now rare to see a woman hand-spinning.

79 *A full spindle of hand-spun cotton, together with a ball of indigo and indigo-dyed cotton yarn. Nigeria.*

A very light spindle is used for spinning cotton by hand. The shaft is from 9 to 12 in (22 to 30 cm) in length, with a small, round, hand-painted ceramic whorl near the bottom. It is usual to support the spindle on a piece of calabash, potsherd or shell, because the short length of the cotton fibres is hardly capable of supporting the weight of the spindle if the drop-and-spin method is used. To quote from Rattray's *Religion and Art in Ashanti* (1927),

The unspun cotton is held on the distaff in the left hand, the sticks of the spindle wetted with spittle, a strand of cotton stuck upon it, and the spindle is set revolving with a twist of the thumb and forefinger. The spindle generally revolves upon a concave fragment of a smooth snail shell. The thread is teased out and twisted into a uniform thickness by the revolving spindle assisted by the fingers of the right hand, which run deftly up and down the teased-out cotton (p. 221).

One way to prepare the cotton for spinning is to open up a boll with the fingers, gently pulling the fibres away from the seeds while at the same time slightly extending the mass of fibres so that it is ready for use. A more methodical way involves first rolling the cotton bolls between an iron rod and a board to squeeze out the seeds and then, having collected a pile of such deseeded bolls, 'bowing' the fibres; that is, plucking a stretched thong over the pile. This has the effect of fluffing up and separating the fibres, ready for spinning.

Hand-spun yarns add a unique character to the surface, feel and handle of a cloth – a notable quality in cloths from Nigeria and Sierra Leone, for example. The abandonment of hand-spun yarns in favour of machine-spun cotton, acrylic, rayon and metallic threads has resulted in the production of harder and more garish cloths. A living tradition, however, does not stand still and the making of cloth as a medium of expression is still very much alive.

80 *Ginning. The seeds are squeezed out between the board and iron rod. Igbetti, Nigeria.*

81 *Dyers in western Nigeria preparing wood-ash water. Ash and water are put in the top pot and the mixture drips down into the lower one. The pots are sunk into old exhausted ash.*

Dyes

Sheep's wool, goat and camel hairs, cotton and silk all produce different shades of colour in their natural state, and these are exploited in much of the weaving in West Africa.

Natural plant dyes are also used; for example, a red dye could be extracted from cassava roots, brown from cola nut, and beige from mango bark. The most important dye, without doubt, is the blue of indigo. The indigo is collected not only from leaves of *Indigofera*, known across the world for its colouring matter, but also from the leaves of a local shrub, *Lonchocarpus cyanescens*. Both species are similar in that they contain indican, a natural glucoside formed in plants which yield indigo. Indican is insoluble in water but converts into a soluble compound, indoxyl, in an alkaline solution; in this case a wood-ash solution.

There are, therefore, several processes in the production of indigo. These can vary in detail in different parts of the country, although in essence they remain the same.

1 The leaves are picked and crushed by pounding in a mortar, after which they are rolled into balls and left to dry in the sun.

2 Green wood is collected, cut up, and burned in specially constructed ovens to produce wood ash. This ash is dampened with spent dye-bath water and likewise formed into balls and left to dry in the sun. Both the dried indigo and the wood-ash balls can be stored away for future use, or, if surplus to the dyers' requirements, sold in the market.

3 Two special earthenware pots are set up one above the other. The top pot has perforations in the base which are covered with a bed of twigs or some sponge to act as a sieve. The potash balls are laid on top, and water poured over them. The water drips through the potash into the pot below, turning alkaline in the process.

4 The lower pot contains pieces of broken-up dye stuff and, in some cases, chopped up roots of *Morinda lucida*, 'the better to fix it' (Teye, 1960).

5 When the pot is filled to the top with the alkaline solution, it is left for five days (being stirred daily), after which it is ready for use. By this time the indigo will have been reduced to a colourless liquid, although the vat is covered with a dark blue froth formed by contact with the oxygen in the air. The goods to be dyed are alternately dipped in the dye vat and oxidated in the air until the desired colour is obtained.

82 In many parts of West Africa indigo dyeing is done by women, but in northern Nigeria – in Kano for instance, where the traveller can still buy deep blue lengths of cloth – the dyeing is done by men in dye pits sunk into the ground.

82 *Dyeing with indigo. Two women are working their dye pots, while dyed cotton skeins dry on sticks in the ground. Two pestles used for pounding the* Lonchocarpus *leaves hang under the roof. Western Nigeria.*

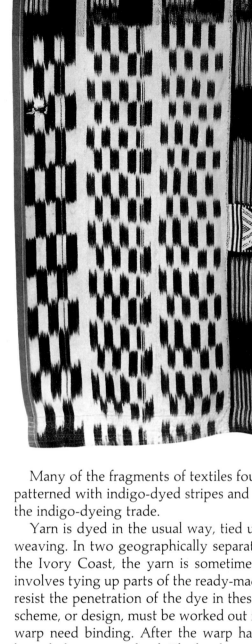

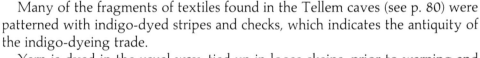

83 Ikat *cloth from the Ivory Coast.*
Basle, Museum für Völkerkunde.

84 *Skein of* ikat-*dyed yarn.*
British Museum.

Many of the fragments of textiles found in the Tellem caves (see p. 80) were patterned with indigo-dyed stripes and checks, which indicates the antiquity of the indigo-dyeing trade.

Yarn is dyed in the usual way, tied up in loose skeins, prior to warping and weaving. In two geographically separated centres of West Africa, Nigeria and the Ivory Coast, the yarn is sometimes resist-dyed by the *ikat* method. This involves tying up parts of the ready-made warp with a bast material, in order to resist the penetration of the dye in these areas, prior to dressing the loom. The scheme, or design, must be worked out first in order to know which parts of the warp need binding. After the warp has been made and the designated parts bound, the warp is dyed. The binding material is removed to reveal the natural colour of the yarn underneath. The warp is then threaded through the heddles and the reed, and mounted on the loom. Due to the inevitable movement of the threads during this process, the sharp divisions of colour get shifted, resulting in the familiar blurred edges. The indigo-dyed cotton cloths from the Ivory Coast, of which there are many examples in the Museum für Völkerkunde, Basle, are perfect examples of this art.

Weaving

Within the confines of the narrow strips woven by men in West Africa a microcosm of textile techniques is found. The design of textiles involves many choices: choice of yarn; colour arrangement of warp; colour arrangement of weft; fabric structure; and additional patterning of warp or weft. In the two preceding chapters the techniques used were limited: the Navaho rugs described are plain weave weft-faced fabrics, while the bedouin use only two basic techniques in addition to plain weave: twining and pick-up weaves. West African narrow-strip weaving, however, involves a variety of techniques.

WARP-FACED TEXTILES

On the whole the strips are warp-faced, although in certain areas the tradition is for weft-faced fabrics. Technically it is easier to keep a consistent width on a narrow fabric if it is warp-faced, as the warp threads lie compactly together, almost four times as many to the inch as for tabby weave; in addition a warp-faced cloth is quicker to weave, which, in view of the length of the warps, could be quite a consideration.

Having chosen a warp-faced plain weave, the next consideration is the colour of the warp. Wool, silk and cotton are sometimes used undyed, but it is more usual to use dyed yarn. If the warp is of one colour only, the plain colour may be broken up by rows of holes. The Yoruba in Nigeria sometimes do this either by inserting a thick pronged comb which distorts the position of the threads, leaving holes — albeit in a rather temporary fashion, as they gradually work out with wear. Alternatively, permanent holes can be made by weaving a series of small slits in which the individual wefts are pulled tight: this exaggerates the slits, turning them into holes. Sometimes the wefts used for forming the slits are carried up over the intervening ground weave until they are needed again, adding yet another decorative feature, as these are shown on the front of the textile and not hidden on the reverse as might be expected.

Most of the textiles introduce different colours into their warps, resulting in striped fabrics. These vary in complexity from a simple contrasting stripe down the centre of a plain ground to combinations of wide and narrow stripes in one colour (often indigo) on a white ground and to multi-coloured stripes.

85 Rows of woven slits have been introduced into this textile of silk yarns.
British Museum.

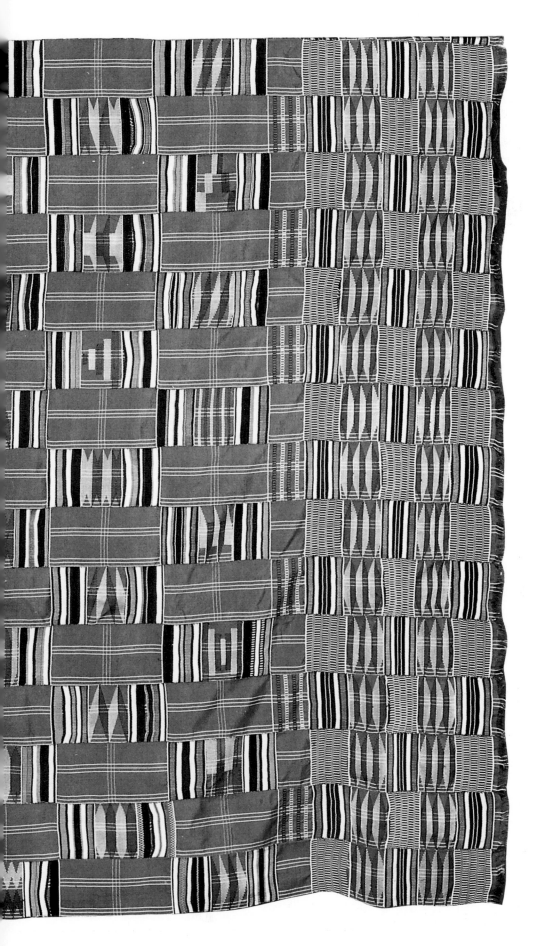

86 *Kente cloth, Asante people, Ghana. A superb cloth of rayon and silk in purple, green and yellow. Compare the symmetrical arrangement of blocks of supplementary patterns, producing a basket-work effect, with the asymmetrical arrangement in the Ewe cloth, Fig. 89.*
British Museum.

Each colour arrangement has a name. This may relate to an important event, a person or a particular group of people; it may be associated with a proverb, or intended to provoke a special feeling or emotion (see Teye, 1960).

In one specific Asante cloth, known as the Liar's cloth, a few very narrow stripes, made up of two to four coloured warp ends on one side of a plain coloured ground, suddenly change sides by way of the weft to continue in the warp on the other side: it was said to have been designed to 'confute persons of doubtful veracity' who came before the Asantehene (Rattray, 1927, p. 244).

WEFT-FACED TEXTILES

In weft-faced textiles the warp threads are set further apart, allowing the weft to bed down, completely covering the warp. The woollen blankets of Mali and the Upper Volta fall into this category, some with strong chequer-board designs interspersed with colourful pattern areas.

Cotton blankets from Sierra Leone and the Ivory Coast use tapestry techniques, sometimes quite freely building up asymmetrical shapes and exploiting all the colour-and-weave effects associated with weft-faced textiles.

WARP- AND WEFT-FACED TEXTILES COMBINED

Not content with the large variety of colourful warp-faced stripes, many weavers go on to cover the stripes completely with areas of weft-face by employing a second pair of shafts which move the threads up and down four or six at a time, instead of one at a time as on the ground weave (see diagram). By treating several fine warp ends as a single unit, a warp-faced textile is converted into a weft-faced one as described above. It is the combining of these two principles that has led to the extraordinary flowering of textile techniques in West Africa, particularly those of the Asante and Ewe.

87

87 Threading for Kente cloth. The small black squares represent individual warps threaded through heddles on the front two shafts alternately. (One row represents one shaft.) The black bars represent six warps threaded together through one heddle alternately on the back pair of shafts.
The lower diagram shows an alternative way of achieving the same result using a conventional four-shaft loom.

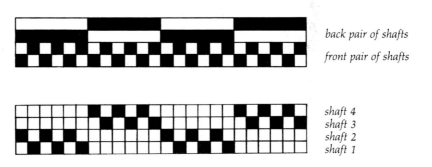

back pair of shafts
front pair of shafts

shaft 4
shaft 3
shaft 2
shaft 1

There are differences in the weaving of the Asante and the Ewe: the Asante use primary colours, reds and yellows being very dominant, while the Ewe use more subdued colours. The rectangular patterns of the Asante are regularly balanced; the Ewe patterns and realistic motifs are more haphazardly distributed. Since the Ewe also imitated the popular Asante cloths, the technical details that follow will be described in general terms. For a detailed analysis of the differences, the reader must turn to *West African Weaving* by Venice Lamb.

86
89

In combining warp and weft faces in one textile, three different methods are used. The first, which shall be called 'weft-faced blocks', uses the second pair of shafts to lift up, for example, alternate groups of six warp threads. These blocks are woven in bands of colour, giving horizontal stripes across the width of the

90

The art of the loom

strip, or are woven in two alternating and contrasting colours, giving vertical stripes. In both cases the weft colours completely obscure the warp stripes, and, if thicker yarn is used, as is sometimes done for the borders, the material becomes considerably thicker.

The second method uses a supplementary weft and both pairs of shafts, the back pair for lifting the threads in groups and the front pair for weaving the ground in tabby. Between every row of pattern weft there are two rows of ground weave. The possible colour sequences are similar to the weft-faced blocks, but the tabby rows in between the pattern rows allow the warp stripes to show through the weft, forming checks.

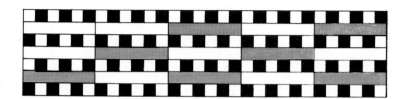

■ ground weave, warp lifted

▦ brocading weft float

88 Diagram showing ground weave alternating with the first three rows of a brocaded motif.

The third method, 'brocade' weaving, also uses a supplementary weft, but in smaller areas, travelling not from selvedge to selvedge but only to the edges of the motif. Many geometrical motifs are used, and, like the stripes, each has its name and association. Sometimes the motif appears in a solid colour because the brocading weft has been inserted twice after every row of ground weave, but in other cases it has a translucent appearance because it is inserted only once between each row.

The Ewe, in addition to the geometrical designs, use representational motifs; a variety of simple designs depicting animals, insects, figures and objects scattered over a plain, rather than a striped, ground, all woven on their side and therefore 'travelling' in the direction of the warp, with charming results.

ASASIA CLOTHS

There remains one important group of textiles, the Asasia cloths, royal cloths of the Asante reserved exclusively for the use of the Asantehene.

Three pairs of shafts were needed for this weaving because the weft stripes and brocaded motifs were woven in twill, which is easily recognised by the diagonal lines running across the patterns. The pair of shafts nearest to the weaver, one and two, would be used for the tabby ground weave as before, but the four remaining shafts would have four or six ends threaded through each individual heddle, threading in sequence one heddle from shaft three, four, five and six respectively and repeating this sequence with all the warp threads. These four shafts would then be lifted in sequence in pairs when inserting the brocading weft.

Note that this last paragraph is written in the past tense. Although there are schemes afoot to keep alive the traditions of weaving in West Africa, it seems unlikely that these sophisticated Asasia cloths will be woven again, for, as Mrs Lamb writes in *West African Weaving*, 'it is a tragic fact that the one remaining weaver alive in Bonwire at the time of writing (May 1972) who remembers the Asasia patterns is no longer capable of weaving them.'

89 (overleaf, left) *Ewe patterned cloth, showing the irregular arrangement of weft-faced blocks and brocaded motifs. British Museum.*

90 (overleaf, right) *Detail of an Asante cloth showing weft-faced blocks completely obscuring the warp with stripes and vertical bars; also supplementary weft stripes with the background showing through (giving the appearance of checks), and two kinds of brocaded motifs: supplementary brocading weft used twice in every row, similar to tapestry, and once in alternate rows, giving a translucent quality. Private collection.*

4 SOUTH-EAST ASIA
Indonesian textiles

The Republic of Indonesia (formerly known as the Dutch East Indies) is made up of thousands of islands lying either side of the equator, forming a link between the peninsula of Malaya in the north-east and Australia in the south-west. The large islands in the north, Sumatra, Java, Bali and Borneo (now known as Kalimantan), rest on a great submerged shallow bank, less than 100 fathoms deep, suggesting that it was once part of the continent to the north; New Guinea lies on the Australian landshelf to the south while the rest of the islands rise out of a sea over 2000 fathoms deep.

Many islands form part of a volcanic chain, the resulting volcanic ash producing rich, fertile soil. These are therefore the most populated islands, Java having the largest population of all. These fertile islands with their wealth of vegetation became a focus of attention for the trading nations of the world from earliest times, particularly for the spices that grew there and were so necessary to disguise the none-too-fresh produce for the table: nutmeg, cinnamon, peppers and cloves. Such cargoes rich in value but small in volume were ideally suited to the precarious sea trade of the times.

Although they were open to cultural and religious influences from north, south, east and west, the remoteness of the smaller islands and the inaccessibility of the interior of the larger ones, particularly Borneo, meant that each island also retained much of its own culture and customs. As a result, the textiles produced in the islands of Indonesia have a richness and diversity which make them some of the most outstanding in the world. Although there are similarities which make an Indonesian textile easily recognisable, it is also possible to assign a textile not only to the specific island where it was made, but even to a particular region of that island.

The textiles of Indonesia represent far more than articles of clothing or material for use in the home. Many of them are imbued with social and religious significance which goes beyond their practical requirements. Although the Indonesians came under the influence successively of Hinduism and Buddhism from the fifth century, followed by Islam in the twelfth to thirteenth centuries, and to a certain extent Christianity in the seventeenth century, their underlying animism (the belief that all living things, including animals and plants, are invested with a soul, and that inanimate objects are endowed with spirits) was never supplanted. They are an easy-going rather than dogmatic people, and gently adapt each successive religion to blend with their own intrinsic beliefs.

In view of the important part textiles play in the life of the Indonesians, the time taken in their preparation is immaterial, and may run into years rather than weeks or months. Time is not equated with money, as it is in the West: material needs are small, but ceremonial textiles are important and represent wealth and prestige to the owner, therefore no time or care must be spared in their production.

Some of the most important, and technically interesting, textiles are the so-called ship cloths formerly woven in south Sumatra, although not now for many

91 *Ceremonial ship cloth from Kroë, south Sumatra. A tampan woven in suppplementary weft on a plain ground weave. London, Victoria and Albert Museum.*

The art of the loom

years: these are long, horizontal rectangular wall hangings, called *palepai*, depicting highly stylised ships. These ships, with high prows at each end and central cabins one above another, contain rows of abstract figures and animals, sometimes even a tree of life. *Palepai* were treasured heirlooms, hung up by their owners at ceremonies of birth and naming, circumcision, marriage and death, indeed at all 'rites of passage' celebrations, which the boat symbolised.

34   Similar small square cloths called *tampan*, woven in the same area but more common than the large *palepai*, also depicted the ship motif. They were used for covering bowls or stools in the same ceremonies.

91   The detailed designs on the *palepai* and *tampan* were woven with a coloured supplementary weft on a plain coloured background, a technique used on other textiles such as the rich gold or silk patterning on sarongs from Bali, Sumatra and Sumbawa. A more unusual technique is the use of supplementary warp threads to depict humans, animals and skull trees, decorating the hem of skirts on the island of Sumba.

There is no doubt that if any one textile skill is connected more firmly with Indonesia than any other country it is the art of dyeing, which the Indonesians have brought to perfection in their *ikats* and batiks. The word *ikat* comes from the stem of the Indonesian word *ingikat*, meaning 'to bind', and is used to describe all the textiles where the designs have been bound with bast material to resist the penetration of the dye in the warp and/or the weft *before* the cloth is woven. These *ikats* are made throughout the islands, but particularly well known are the blankets and jackets woven by the Iban people of northern Borneo, in Sarawak (now part of Malaysia). Anthropomorphic, animal or abstract designs are crammed into a central field between narrow stripes at the selvedges; sometimes
93   figures are ranged in rows (as in the jacket illustrated), and sometimes various elements of design are interlocked in complex forms.

Other *ikats*, from the island of Sumba, also range the motifs in rows but not on
92   a plain background: on bands of bright orange, deep blue and black, some wide, others narrow, motifs of sea-horses, deer, skull trees and full-frontal male nudes are repeated in mirror images across the width of the cloth.

Ikat and batik, another dyeing technique, in which wax and other resists are applied to the already woven cloth before dyeing, are two popular crafts practised in the West but still referred to in their original language: perhaps it will not be long before *ikat* joins batik in some English dictionaries.

The loom

Although a treadle loom is sometimes used in workshops in the islands, all the significant weaving referred to in the foregoing pages is done on the back-strap loom (also known as the body-tension loom). The terms 'back-strap' and 'body-tension' both accurately describe the ancient and primitive loom used by Indonesian women.

The tension needed on all looms to keep the warp threads taut and in parallel order is supplied by the weaver's body. She sits on the ground with the warp beam attached by cords to a fixed point, or fitted into a pair of supports at one end, and the breast beam at the other, almost in her lap. The latter is kept in place by a support which goes around her back, sitting comfortably on her hips, and attached to each end of the beam by cords. Her slightest body movements

92 *A shoulder cloth from Sumba, with figures and animals depicted in warp* ikat. *Private collection.*

93 *A Dyak man's coat from
Sarawak, North Borneo: warp ikat
of anthropomorphic figures.
British Museum.*

control the tension of the warp: a movement forward slackens the tension, facilitating the lifting of the threads to make the shed, and a movement back tightens the tension, making it easier to beat the weft home.

There are two different versions of the back-strap loom as used in Indonesia: the circular warp loom and the discontinuous warp loom. The circular warp loom almost certainly pre-dates the discontinuous warp loom (Gittinger, 1979b, p. 13) and will be described first.

THE CIRCULAR WARP LOOM
A warp is prepared which is just a little over half the length of the finished cloth, allowance being made for the 'take-up' in weaving. ('Take-up' describes the physical property of threads undulating over and under each other, rather than travelling on a straight plane.) The warp is made on a special frame with removable slats at the top and bottom. While making the warp, the yarn is passed alternately over and under two cords stretched across the frame and level with the top layer of threads. Later, after the warp has been taken off and dyed, it is stretched between the two beams that constitute the loom, and laze rods inserted in place of the cords to preserve the cross made while warping. The warp appears to be approximately half the finished length because it circulates around the two beams without being attached at any point, the weaving taking place on the top layer of threads nearest to the weaver and the finished cloth being moved down and under the breast beam as work progresses.

The laze rods help to keep the warp threads in order, and also define the two

4

94 *Weaving ceremonial* hinggi *cloth on a back-strap loom with a continuous circulating warp. Clearly visible, starting from the front, are the breast beam, tenterhook, sword, heddle rod and shed rod. Prailiu village, Sumba.*

sets of threads needed to form the shed for weaving. One of these sets of threads will have a continuous heddle encircling each individual thread to attach it to the heddle bar, so that all the threads can be lifted up together when the heddle bar is raised. The alternate threads go over a shed rod to produce the counter-shed.

The warp beam is attached to two posts on the veranda of the weaver's home, or two suitable trees outside in the shade, at a height slightly above the breast beam, which is virtually in the weaver's lap.

The back strap consists of the support for the weaver's back with attachments to secure it to each end of the breast beam. The support is made variously of bark, wood or bast fibre, usually lined with some form of padding and sometimes elaborately carved with fretsaw designs. A spool to carry the weft and a sword to beat the weft home complete the equipment necessary to weave a simple piece of cloth. For the more complex weaves, for example the supplementary warp weaves, many additional pick-up sticks (*lidi*) are inserted in the warp to select the particular warp threads to be lifted for each row of the design.

An interesting variation on the warping and dressing of the loom, in which a second warp beam (or coil rod) is used in place of the laze rods, is described in detail by Rita Bolland (1971, pp. 149–57 and 171–9) and also compared with the discontinuous warp loom.

The circular warp loom is used in many circumstances: to weave the warp-faced cloths of a more or less standard length such as those woven by the Iban of northern Borneo; for the *kain grinsing*, the double-*ikat* sacred cloth woven in the village of Tenganan Pagringsingan on the island of Bali, where a circular cloth is essential to the ritual in which the cutting of the warp threads has symbolic meaning; and in other warp-cutting ceremonies such as that which attends a child's first hair-cut.

THE DISCONTINUOUS WARP LOOM

The circular warp loom has its limitations in that the length of the warp is restricted because there is a limit to the weight of the threads it is possible to stretch out between two points. The discontinuous warp loom introduces two additional features. First, a flat board on which a long warp can be wound, and which is held in a specially made support; and second, a reed to keep the warp threads regularly spaced – a great advantage for weaving balanced fabrics such as the simple tartans striped in both warp and weft, and the ground weave for the patterned supplementary weft weaves. The warp can now be made any length and wrapped around the board before it is placed in the support, positioned about 3 ft (1 m) away from where the weaver sits.

The reed, constructed of slivers of cane kept rigid in a frame, is threaded with the ends of the warp before being attached to the breast beam: this keeps the threads evenly spaced throughout the weaving. Strangely enough, the sword beater is still used to beat the weft into position; in other parts of the world the reed takes the place of the sword (Ling Roth, 1977, p. 77).

Within these two basic types of loom there are variations. The discontinuous warp loom is sometimes used without a reed, and some textiles are woven with as many as three heddle bars in addition to the many pattern sticks. As Rita Bolland points out in her comparison of the looms used in Bali and Lombak, 'there is a relation between the function of the finished cloth and the type of loom on which it is woven' (1971, p. 177).

95 *The discontinuous warp loom. The long warp is wound on to the warp board, which is held in position by two wooden supports. The back support is attached to the breast beam by cords at each end.*

Spinning

Thomas Stamford Raffles, after whom the famous hotel in Singapore was named, and one of the first writers on Indonesian textiles, wrote,

It is part of the domestic economy, that the women of the family should provide the men with cloths necessary for their apparel, and from the consort of the sovereign to the wife of the lowest peasant, the same rule is observed. In every cottage there is a spinning-wheel and loom, and in all ranks a man is accustomed to pride himself on the beauty of a cloth woven by his wife, mistress, or daughter (1817, p. 95).

This is far from the truth now, but the spinning wheel is still in use for spinning locally grown cotton. The cotton grown on the Indonesian islands is the shrubby *Gossypium arboreum*, and is both cultivated on a domestic scale and found growing wild in the hedges.

A small hand-operated gin is used for removing the seeds. The cotton bolls are fed through two easily adjusted rotating rollers which hold back the seeds while letting the cotton go through. The cotton fibres are then either bowed (as

96 *Spinning with the rimless wheel. The spinner sits on the ground, turning the handle with her right hand and drawing out the cotton fibres with her left.*

described in the chapter on West African weaving) or beaten with rattan beaters into a mat of fibres which can then be rolled up into finger-sized rolls ready for spinning.

The spinning wheel consists of two pairs of uprights, a small delicate pair and a large stout pair, set each end of a flat board. The small uprights support the horizontal spindle which rotates freely in bearings; the large uprights support the rimless wheel, which is made from a pair of six- or eight-pronged supports attached at either end of the axle and turned by a protruding handle. The tips of the prongs are interlaced to form a support for the drive band. The drive band connects the wheel with the spindle, and when the wheel is turned, the spindle rotates at speed.

The spinner sits on the ground, turning the handle with her right hand and drawing out the fibres with her left. The forming cotton thread is held at an obtuse angle to the spindle, the yarn slipping off the tip as the spindle rotates. When the spinner has fully extended the roll with her left arm and can reach no further, she turns the handle in the opposite direction in order to back off the yarn so that it is at right angles to the spindle, after which she can again reverse the direction of the wheel and wind on the length of yarn just spun. Spinning and winding are continued alternately until the spindle is full. The spun cotton is then slipped off the spindle and wound into balls ready for plying. The plied yarn is wound on to a skein-winder prior to starching or dyeing.

Cotton is used more than any other fibre on the Indonesian islands, but silk also has an important part to play, especially on festive occasions. It is not spun like cotton but reeled and thrown on improvised equipment. The cocoons of the silk moth *Bombyx mori* are floated in a basin of hot water to soften the sericin, the natural gum that binds the threads together. The ends of several cocoons are taken up together and wound on to a reel forming one very fine thread. The throwing consists of taking several of these fine threads and twisting them together, the number of turns per inch or centimetre giving anything from a soft lustrous to a crepe yarn. Sericulture is practised on some of the islands, but silk is also imported from India and China. A variey of silk cloths are found on the island of Bali, for example the weft *ikats* and the decorative silk cloths with supplementary weft patterning. The Bugis villagers of Tajunca in southern Celebes (now known as Sulawesi) have a thriving cottage industry in weaving silk weft *ikats*, described in detail by Wanda Warming and Michael Gaworski, who travelled extensively around Southeast Asia and Indonesia gathering material for their book (1981, pp. 114–20).

Raffles also refers to a fibre made from the leaves of the pineapple plant, sometimes called 'silk grass', and described in detail in a book on textile fibres: 'It is very fine in staple and highly lustrous, and is white, soft, and flexible. It is used in the manufacture of the celebrated *pina* cloth . . . and was considered to be the most delicate in structure of any known vegetable fiber' (Matthews, 1904, p. 823). This, together with many bast fibres, is certainly used in the Indonesian islands. After softening in water, the fibres are split with the nails and knotted together end to end for use as warp and weft. The knots are so tiny that they can hardly be seen (Ross, 1988, p. 139).

Dyes

Although chemical dyes have been introduced in Indonesia, as elsewhere in the world, it seems that the importance that has always been attached to the actual preparation and processes of using natural dyes in the past still holds good today. In a strange way the new and the old go hand in hand. For example, the Iban in Sarawak use earthy red-browns obtained from natural dyes as the background colour for their *ikat* designs, but add plain narrow warp strips of vivid yarns in commercially dyed colours either side. Perhaps it is that the use of natural dyes seems inexorably linked with the *ikat*-ing processes; tying up the designs to be reserved on the warp threads takes such a long time, and the consequent dyeing is considered such an important part of the final product, that merely opening a packet of powder could not possibly fulfil the role.

The *ikat* technique is known all over the world, but its origins were in Indonesia (Buhler, 1942, p. 1604). The first *ikats*, and the most numerous, are the warp *ikats* in which only the warp threads are dyed with designs: the weft thread, although coarser, is invisible because the structure of the textile is a warp-faced plain weave, the warp ends being set so closely together that they completely cover the weft. This shows off the design to the greatest advantage because, if the threads were further apart and the weft showed through between them, it would interfere with the clarity of the design.

The designs of *ikats* repeat themselves on a vertical or horizontal axis, sometimes on both. In order to facilitate the tying-up of the design elements in

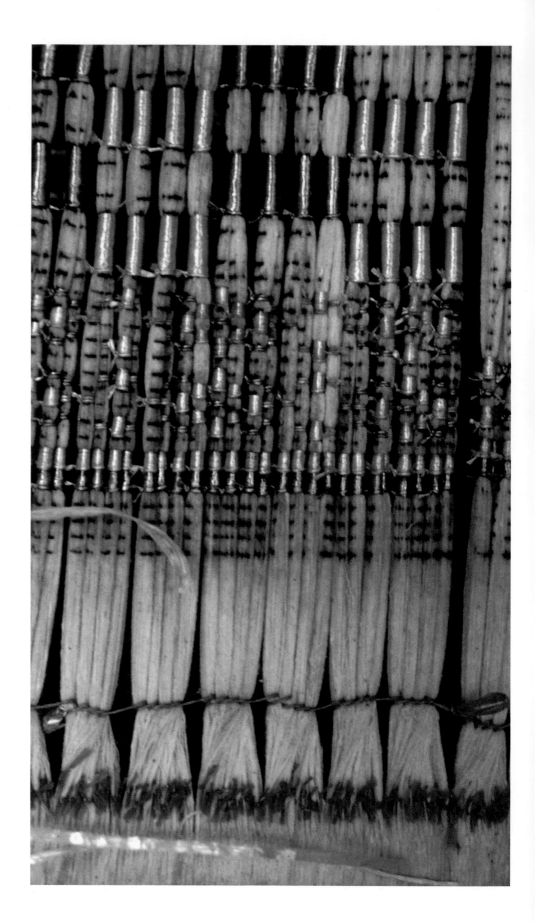

97 *The warp divided into sets and bound with plastic 'Jap-tie' before dyeing. Tenganan, Bali.*

The art of the loom

the warp, the warp threads are arranged in such a manner that all the repeats of the design are bound at once. The warp is wound on a special apparatus and the cross, which separates the even from the uneven threads, is secured in the usual way. After inserting the cross, the warp threads are divided into 'sets', small units of from six to ten threads which will always be treated as one. When these have been secured, the whole set of warp threads is folded over on itself, reducing the width by half, or each side is folded in one-third, reducing the width to a third of the original. The sets of threads of the new layers are now incorporated with the original sets, the work of tying-up having been reduced by one-half or one-third. If, in addition, the design is to be repeated from top to bottom as well as from side to side, as with the warps made for the circular warp loom, then the number of layers dealt with in one go are doubled and the two layers become four, and the three layers become six.

The design is roughly marked out on the warp threads after they have been mounted on the *ikat*-ing frame, and all the parts to be left undyed are bound first, using bast material (or more recently plastic 'Jap-tie') to resist the dye. Next the parts to be dyed red are bound, and sometimes marked with an extra knot so that they are easily recognisable. The warp is then dyed in the indigo bath as many times as is needed to produce the required tone of blue, or, if strong enough, black. When dry, the warp is put back on the tying frame and the bound areas to be dyed red are removed. After dyeing with red, the remaining bindings are removed and the whole stretched until dry. If the indigo was dyed to a medium tone of blue as part of the colour scheme, it would in turn have to be covered with binding material before being immersed in the red dye, otherwise the blue would be overprinted with the red, producing the dark purple found in the background colour of many *ikats*.

Blue and red are the two most important colours used, the blue of indigo and the red of *mengkudu*. Dyeing with indigo has already been described in Chapter 3 on West African narrow-strip weaving and, although some ingredients and methods of procedure may differ in detail, it is not necessary to describe it again here. However, the dyeing of the *mengkudu* colour (from the outside layers of the roots of *Morinda citrifolia*, a wild-growing member of the *Rubiaceae* family) introduces an interesting new dyeing procedure.

The colouring matter alizarin, obtained from the roots, is the same as the colouring matter in the roots of madder. The simple method of dyeing wool with madder, with alum as a mordant, was described in Chapter 2 on the bedouin. Dyeing with madder on cotton fibres is a very different matter, and was perfected in the Middle East in turkey red dyeing. It is this long and involved method which has been carried eastwards and adapted for dyeing with *mengkudu*.

The cotton fibres do not take up the colouring matter easily unless they are subjected to a rigorous pre-dyeing treatment. The yarns to be dyed are worked in a mixture of wood ash and oil. The lye water strained off the wood ash is mixed with oil, animal fat or crushed nuts, and rubbed into the previously boiled and dried yarn. Other ingredients are sometimes included: crushed roots containing tannin or the yellow substantive dye *Curcuma* (turmeric). The yarn is dried between repeated dippings and is sometimes worked with the feet. This preliminary treatment, incidentally, gives a warm background colour to the yarn in the design which will remain undyed.

For the dyeing, small parts of the roots of the *mengkudu* tree are pounded to a powder with a pestle in a mortar, together with bark containing alumina, and all mixed with water. The yarns are immersed in the dye bath overnight, rinsed in the morning and hung out to dry. This can be repeated as often as is necessary to dye to the depth of colour required. Some of the many variations on this basic recipe, practised in different parts of the archipelago, are described by Warming and Gaworski (1981, pp. 69–71), though others may have been omitted, their details a closely guarded secret.

Reds can also be obtained from other natural sources: from the dye retrieved from the resinous secretions of the lac shield louse and used for dyeing silk; from annatto, obtained from the pulp surrounding the seeds of *Bixa orellana*; and from the boiled bark of the mangrove tree.

Other woods, roots and leaves produce yellows, rusts and browns when used with mordants, aluminium or tannin-bearing plants, or ferruginous mud for black.

A. Bühler in *Dyes and Dyeing Methods for Ikat Threads* (1942, p. 1602) writes,

It is difficult to secure reliable information as to the duration of the various processes of which the making of an ikat *is composed. Some details have, however, been collected in various parts of Indonesia. On the islands of Rote more than a year is taken up by the three dyeings. In central Flores the entire labour, from picking the cotton to weaving the fabric, is, according to Scheller, accomplished in three months. This does not include dyeing which requires between six and eight years.*

This was many years ago, but even Warming and Gaworski writing in the 1980s say, 'the length of time needed to complete the dyeing . . . can take more than one year' (1981, p. 69).

Weaving

PLAIN WEAVE

Ikats are woven in plain weave or an extended plain weave, that is, over two, under two, instead of over one, under one. In the warp-faced *ikats* the threads are set close together as already mentioned, but there are also weft-faced and double *ikats*, both a speciality of the island of Bali. The warp threads on the weft-faced *ikats* are set further apart, allowing the weft to cover the warp completely; the double *ikats* have a balanced set so that both sets of threads show equally. Plain cotton materials striped in the warp and banded in the weft making colourful tartans are also woven in a plain balanced weave.

SUPPLEMENTARY WEFT

Some of the most exciting textiles from Indonesia are the patterned and pictorial cloths woven with a contrasting supplementary weft on a plain ground weave. The supplementary weft skips over several of the ground warps, picking out the design row by row. The selected warp threads are picked up on *lidi* sticks, all of them sometimes being placed in position before the weaving commences. These sticks lie ready in order at the far end of the warp and are brought forward one at a time to be replaced by the sword; the sword is turned on edge to produce a wider gap through which to pass the stick shuttle on which the weft thread is wound. The ground weave warp threads are lifted by two heddle rods used alternately, and one or two rows are woven between each row of supplementary weft. Specific groups of supplementary weft textiles are described below.

Songket   The *songket* cloths are woven in silk or very fine cotton with small floral or geometric repeat patterns in metallic threads. Real gold or silver would formerly have been used for the supplementary weft, and the decorative cloths were kept for wear on ceremonial occasions at court and at weddings.

Songket are woven on many of the Indonesian islands, and the production of some is described in detail in Warming and Gaworski (1981, pp. 129–34). Of particular interest is the description of a weaver in Bali who, having picked up her design on *lidi* sticks (sometimes as many as two hundred are used) proceeds to replace them all with continuous string heddles. There is much more freedom of use with heddles because the warp threads can be raised by them in any order: when pattern sticks are used, only the front one is operative; all the sticks lying behind are obstructed by the one in front.

Palepai and *Tampan*   *Palepai* are ceremonial wall hangings, measuring about 114 × 24 in (290 × 60 cm), hung horizontally on the wall, the width more than four times the height. They used to be woven on the south coast of Sumatra, and those not still owned by families on the island are now treasured possessions of museums or in private collections. A *palepai* depicts a ship or a pair of ships with curved prows, the ship laden with figures and animals in simplified but recognisable forms. The designs of the two halves of the *palepai* are mirror images of each other and, since so much work was involved in picking up each row of even half the length of the textile, it is tempting to suppose that the *lidi* were stored at the end of the warp until all were used, and then reused in reverse order. This would be possible if each row of supplementary weft was picked up, woven, and the *lidi* pushed to the end. The second pattern row would be picked up,

98 *Replacing* lidi *sticks with continuous string heddles.*

99 Detail of a small cloth
showing the pilih technique, from
Sarawak, North Borneo. The
figures stand out against a
background of red and black
stripes of supplementary weft.
Private collection.

woven, and the *lidi* pushed down to join the first — and so on till the last *lidi* to be inserted would be the first one to be reused. If an obvious mistake in the design appears in exactly the same place on the other half, it proves that this was the way it was done. On some *palepai*, however, although a first glance would seem to support this theory, a closer look reveals all kinds of differences in detail in the two halves.

The ground weave of the *palepai* is natural-coloured cotton; the supplementary weft is of two or three different coloured cottons working backwards and forwards across the parts of the design where the colour is needed, described as using 'discontinuous wefts'.

The fine craftsmanship of the *palepai* is repeated in the *tampan*, small square ceremonial cloths also depicting ships loaded with animals and humans, though some contain simpler abstract designs. The *tampan* illustrated on p. 101 was woven entirely in dark blue, except for a little brown in the border top and bottom. In this case the supplementary weft went from selvedge to selvedge with a continuous weft and the reverse side of the textile shows a negative image of the front. The detail of the *tampan* also shows the device used to break up a large area of flat colour. Little units of two by two of the ground weave are incorporated at regular intervals in the coloured areas, adding a characteristic decorative touch to the textile. The *tampan* illustrated on p. 36 uses two contrasting colours throughout, and the detail of the reverse of the textile shows long skips of weft thread where it jumps from one coloured area to another.

Pilih   The *pilih* technique, confined to the Iban Dyaks of Sarawak, is a supplementary weft technique in which the design elements stand out in ground weave, against red- and black-striped floats in the background.

The word *pilih* means to choose, a term that could be used to describe all the supplementary weft techniques, but is confined to these particular red and black textiles. Haddon and Start (1936, p. 89) describe a similar textile as having 'elaborately embroidered' patterns:

This cloth has an extremely rich effect, produced by embroidered pattern lines of thick red and black wool, and is the only example we have found that has any wool in it. When woven the cloth was white bordered by two composite self-covered stripes with a narrow white stripe between them. The whole of the white portion has been covered by embroidered patterns.

This raises the whole question of how one can tell, from studying a textile in a museum, whether the design has been put in as the cloth is woven (weaving) or added afterwards to an already woven piece of cloth (embroidery). In this case there is more evidence to suggest that the designs are woven with supplementary wefts, but it is possible that some are also done with a needle, decorating the plain cloth after it is woven, perhaps in imitation of the woven designs. There is a child's jacket in the Tropen Museum in Amsterdam with so many short ends of coloured yarn showing on the reverse side that the design could well have been put in with a needle afterwards (a needle holds only a short length of yarn). The *pilih* cloth illustrated here, from a private collection, has no loose ends on the back, and is in fact completely reversible like a *tampan*. The owner is sure that it was woven with a supplementary weft using a continuous length of yarn on a stick shuttle.

100 (overleaf, left) *Detail from the reverse of the ship cloth illustrated in Fig. 91, showing the negative image.* London, Victoria and Albert Museum.

101 (overleaf, right) *Detail from the reverse of the tampan illustrated in Fig. 34. The additional colours used in this textile necessitate a certain amount of skipping from one area to another.*

The art of the loom

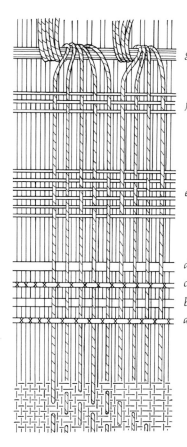

102 *Border of a cloth from Sumba with anthropomorphic figures and skull trees, woven with supplementary warp. British Museum.*

104 (facing page) *Detail of a Sumba cloth (Fig. 35) woven in supplementary warp. London, Victoria and Albert Museum.*

g
f
e
d
c
b
a

103 *Schematic representation of the loom used in weaving supplementary warp borders, after a drawing by Rita Bolland in 'Weaving a Sumba woman's skirt':*
(a) and (c) ground weave heddles;
(b) bamboo stick under alternate ground weave warps and all supplementary warps;
(d) round bamboo under all supplementary warps;
(e) six out of the ninety pattern sticks;
(f) laze rods for the supplementary warps;
(g) bundle of sticks for use in adjusting warp tension.

SUPPLEMENTARY WARP

Another textile technique, no longer practised but of great interest, was reserved for decorative strips to be sewn on to the hems of skirts worn on special occasions on the island of Sumba. The designs were woven with a supplementary warp, a rarer technique than supplementary wefts, which are to be found in many parts of the world.

The thick light-coloured supplementary warps are laid in position over the ground weave ones in the parts where the design is to appear: one supplementary thread to every two ground weave threads. Pattern sticks are threaded through the supplementary warps, selecting the warp threads needed to be raised for each row of the design. The ground weave warp threads are threaded alternately through the two sets of heddles nearest to the weaver. In addition, a bamboo stick is placed between the two heddles over which alternate ground warps and all supplementary warps run.

Weaving commences with a few rows of both sets of warps woven together using the front heddle and the bamboo stick alternately. Thereafter, the two heddle bars are used for the ground weave, one pattern stick brought forward and the warp threads lying over it combined with every two rows of ground weave. As with supplementary weft weaves, there may be as many as a hundred pattern sticks laced into the warp.

A distinctive element in the Sumba designs is the twill formation of the pattern areas. The raised supplementary warp threads are stepped one side to right or left on each successive row, making the typical diagonal lines of a twill structure: the change of direction is used to great effect in the flat areas of the design. The usual problem of long floats on the reverse side arises, and these are dealt with in two ways: either the background area between the larger figures is broken up with many smaller design motifs so that there are no longer any floats; or, where the background is left plain, every 4 inches (10 centimetres) or so an extra weft pick in the background colour catches up the long floating warp threads at the back and ties them into the ground weave.

118   *The art of the loom*

105 *The border of a* ragidup, *a sacred cloth used in gift-exchanging ceremonies. This cloth combines supplementary warps and wefts, ikat and twining, as well as an exchange from dark to light warp in the central panel. Sumatra.*
London, Victoria and Albert Museum.

There are problems with the tension of the supplementary warp threads, as they do not get used up at the same rate as the ground weave warps. This is remedied at the outset by giving the supplementary warp threads, in small groups, a complete turn around a bundle of sticks at the warp beam end of the loom; every time the supplementary warp slackens, another stick or two pushed into the bundle tightens it up.

The description of these decorative borders is based on a full account in *Weaving a Sumba Woman's Skirt* (Bolland, 1956, pp. 49–56), and only differs in the last-mentioned detail, where Rita Bolland suggests that a stick was 'taken out' to slacken the supplementary warps, rather than 'put in' to tighten them. Practical experiment, however, proves that these warps, with far fewer intersections than the ground weave, become slacker rather than tighter.

Lamak Supplementary warps were also used in the weaving of *lamak*, tall banners used by temples in Bali during their new year celebrations. Thick bundles of white supplementary warp threads were used on a dark ground weave, the design showing an hourglass figure at the top with a stylised version of the goddess of rice underneath, and a large field of geometric motifs below that. Usually these banners were made from palm and were of a temporary nature, making the few woven in cotton quite rare.

OTHER TEXTILE TECHNIQUES

Pinatikan The *pinatikan* fabrics were woven in the northern region of the large Indonesian island Celebes. They were not very common and are now only to be found in museums. The cloths were woven in warp-faced stripes on the continuous warp loom, producing a seamless tube. Three of these would be sewn together horizontally to make a skirt.

The characteristic feature of *pinatikan* is the little zig-zag and lozenge-shaped patterns which appear either in alternate stripes or over the whole surface. The patterns were produced by warping two colours together in the patterned areas and, by careful arrangement of heddles and pattern sticks, lifting up different combinations of warp threads to skip over three weft rows, in five pick repeats. The results, if turned through 90°, are very similar to many zig-zag and lozenge-shaped all-over patterns found in European peasant weaving produced on four-shaft looms, but to produce the same effect in a warp-faced weave on such a primitive loom was a very different matter, and took great skill. For a full description of *pinatikan* see 'Weaving the *Pinatikan*' (Bolland, 1977).

Ragidup Perhaps the strangest of all the Indonesian textiles were the *ragidup* (sacred cloths used in gift-exchanging ceremonies) made by the Batak people of Sumatra. They contain no striking figurative motifs to attract the attention as in many of the textiles so far described, yet many varied techniques are combined in one textile.

Basically the cloth is made out of three panels sewn together along their length. The two narrow panels on each side are in warp-faced plain weave with a very narrow band of supplementary warp designs on the inside edges. The central panel has a centre field of dark, striped material with a small *ikat* device between the stripes. Fastened into the last few rows at the top and bottom of this dark, striped panel are new white warp threads on which delicate supplementary weft patterns are woven: the remaining dark warp threads are cut away. Finally, a narrow band of decorative twining completes the two fringed edges.

As a weaver, it is difficult to imagine a more complex textile, combining, as it does, *ikat*, supplementary warp and weft techniques, an exchange of warps, and twining.

5 EAST ASIA, THE ISLANDS OF JAPAN
Kasuri resist dyeing

The previous chapter on Indonesian textiles included many references to *ikats*, resist-dyed fabrics rich in design and full of ritualistic and symbolic importance. The *kasuri* fabrics of Japan are also resist-dyed, but their style and function are quite different. The fabrics are used for working clothes, futon covers and household materials, and the style was developed by peasant farmers and fishermen from two simple ingredients available to them, cotton and indigo. Although other fibres and other dyes are also used, a large proportion of characteristic *kasuri* designs are white on a blue ground.

The word *ikat* comes from the stem of the word *mengikat*, to bind. *Kasuri* comes from the word *kasureru*, meaning to blur; the former thus describes how the effect is achieved, and the latter how it looks. This is significant, for the Japanese use methods other than binding for resisting the dye on the yarns to be used for warp and weft. The translation of Japanese depends on the interpretation of the individual characters, so there are different ways of translating the verb *kasureru*, two of which are quoted by Langewis (1963, p. 77) from the *Encyclopedia Nipponica*: 'in passing touch lightly' or 'lightly brush or stroke along'. They both describe the 'brush stroke' effect of the little repeating geometric motifs which are typical of *kasuri* fabrics. The reasons for the soft ragged edges will become apparent when the methods are described.

Japan is a crescent-shaped archipelago spanning an area from the 45th to the 25th parallel, with consequent variations in climate and agriculture. There are four main islands in the north and a string of smaller ones to the south, the Ryukyu Islands reaching almost to Taiwan.

Through the study of pottery in excavations, it has been possible to determine that as far back as 200 BC rough textiles were woven from nettle fibres, hemp and ramie in the south, and bark fibres in the north. At this time the aboriginal Ainu were joined by the peoples of the mainland, Manchurian, Chinese and Korean; but for long periods of time there was no communication between Japan and the mainland.

In AD 250 there are references to the fact that fabrics woven from the stiffer bark fibres were used for work clothes, and those from the thinner stalk fibres for clothes worn at home. Around AD 500 waves of immigrants from Korea brought with them advanced techniques of manufacture for spinning, weaving and dyeing, and also introduced silk. The new dyeing techniques resulted in more colourful cloth and the appearance of the first *kasuri* dyed fabric (possibly not woven in Japan but brought from China); it does not appear that *kasuri* techniques established themselves at this early date.

From the beginning of the ninth century to the end of the twelfth century the warrior class held power. The 'shoguns', or hereditary commanders-in-chief, encouraged austerity and introduced laws limiting the width of cloth to 15 in (38 cm), which led to plainer clothes being worn. The *kosode* or 'small sleeves' underwear of the former nobility now became the model for the outer garment, the *kimono*.

106 *Silk* kasuri *fabric from the Ryukyu Islands.*

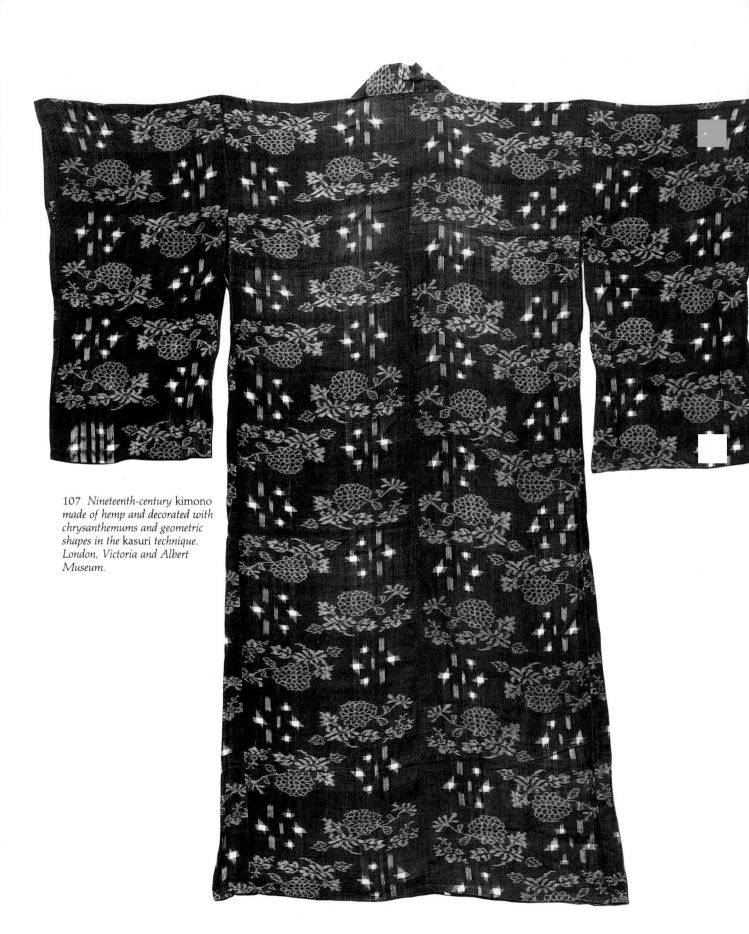

107 Nineteenth-century kimono
made of hemp and decorated with
chrysanthemums and geometric
shapes in the kasuri technique.
London, Victoria and Albert
Museum.

Cotton was introduced into Japan, it is said, by a Portuguese in 1512. It was soon cultivated, and the fibres spun and woven into cloth by almost every housewife in the country. Because of its utility, warmth and strength it was especially taken up by working people. During the Edo period, that is the period spanning two and a half centuries between 1600 and 1868, Japan cut itself off from the rest of the world and, as a result, Europe's seventeenth-century scientific revolution passed it by. There had been considerable trade before this period not only with China and Korea, but with Europe as well (the Far West); but when the Portuguese were ordered to leave in 1639, the Dutch moved to an artificial island in 1641 and even the Chinese segregated to a special compound, the country was, to all intents and purposes, closed down. And so it remained, developing entirely from its own traditions, with only those outside influences which had been absorbed prior to the 1600s and a few new ideas infiltrating through the port of Nagasaki (the only port to remain open during this period), until Commodore Perry of the USA demanded the opening of the ports in 1853–4.

During this time, not only cotton, but indigo-producing dye plants became so popular that both crops were being grown in nearly every village. It was with the rapid increase in cotton weaving and indigo dyeing that the *kasuri* technique developed. It first took hold in Okinawa, the largest of the Ryukyu Islands. It may be that *ikats* from the East Indian islands were brought here as presents or goods for sale by traders as early as the fifteenth century and influenced the islanders' methods of decorating fabrics; others say that the white marks left in a skein tied up too tightly for dyeing first gave people the idea of binding up selected threads. The 'invention' of *kasuri* has even been attributed to a lady in Kurume who noticed, while ravelling her old *kimono*, that at the points of interlacement the colour of the thread was different (Langewis, 1963).

Be that as it may, we know that by the seventeeth century all the women on the island of Kume, for example (one of the smaller of the Ryukyu Islands), had to weave in an official weaving lodge under constant supervision in order to produce seventy percent of taxes paid in silk cloth to the Satsuma clan who ruled the Ryukyu Islands (Mitchell, 1984, p. 16). Even today the 650 weavers on the island of Kume undergo a six-month training period in the Weaving Centre before starting to work in their own homes. As stated in an article on Japanese resist-dyeing techniques (on which much of the foregoing history is based), 'A harsh poll-tax was levied in Okinawa and women everywhere were long obliged to weave large quantities of fabric conforming to very strictly enforced standards. However the system gave home weavers a very thorough training in the textile arts and thus bequeathed to posterity weaving and dyeing techniques which produce fabrics of unparalleled beauty' (*CIBA Review* 1967/4, p. 6).

Yarns

Many vegetable fibres and one animal fibre are used in the weaving of textiles in the Japanese islands. The vegetable fibres include those taken from the bark of trees, the bast fibres from the stems of plants, leaf fibres, and the seed hairs of cotton. The animal fibre is silk.

The variety of fibres is reflected in the range of textiles produced in Japan, of which the *kasuri* fabrics are only a small part. The traditional *kimono*, for instance, may be made in sumptuous brocaded silk woven on a draw-loom, painted, stencilled, embroidered, or embellished in other ways, and kept for special occasions; it may be made in one of the cool bast fibres, collectively known as *asa*, for summer wear; or in cotton, sometimes padded for extra warmth, for work and everyday wear.

The oldest materials used from the start of the millennium were the elm bark fibres woven into short coats by the Ainu, and hemp fibres, which are prepared in a similar way to linen.

All Aino women understand the making of bark cloth. The men bring in the bark in strips, five feet long, having removed the outer coating. This inner bark is easily separated into several thin layers, which are split into very narrow strips by the older women, very neatly knotted, and wound into balls weighing about a pound each. No preparation of either the bark or thread is required to fit it for weaving, but I observe that some of the women steep it in a decoction of a bark which produces a brown dye to deepen the buff tint (Bird, 1880).

Japanese hemp is smooth and glossy, a light straw colour, and extremely fine. It is used not only for clothing and curtains, but also in the making of mosquito nets. 'Once every housewife felt justifiably proud if, in addition to her family's clothing, she managed during her working life to make one whole mosquito net, i.e. a piece of fine hempen mesh 100 metres long and 37 cm wide. It was such green mosquito nets which give Japanese summer scenes their typical fairy-tale atmosphere' (*CIBA Review*, 1967/4, p. 12).

Nettle fibres are also used, to spin another linen-type yarn. 'At the Paris Exposition in 1878 Japan exhibited a large collection of nettle fibres, yarns, and fabrics' (Matthews, 1924, p. 832). Paper mulberry fibres are also employed; the sheets of paper are cut into narrow strips, twisted into yarn and used as weft in much the same way as rags are used in the West. Arrowroot fibres, ramie and banana fibres are also made into yarns, this wide variety perhaps saying something about both the range of indigenous plants in the many islands of Japan and the ingenuity of the people. To begin with, they used the materials they found growing wild, and then proceeded to cultivate and improve the strains of those plants which were proving most useful to them and best suited to the environment.

Cotton, the dominant fibre in Japan, was introduced in the sixteenth century and immediately proved popular. But as the preparation of cotton has already been described in the chapters on West Africa and Indonesia, it is more useful here to describe in detail the production of silk yarns.

The first silk came from wild silkworms feeding on the leaves of oak and chestnut trees growing in the mountain forests. The silk produced was the light brown variety we call tussah. Although the mulberry tree, on which the cultivated silkworm feeds, is indigenous to Japan, sericulture was not introduced until the third century when, according to legend, a secret mission captured four Chinese girls (or persuaded the girls to accompany them) and brought them back to Japan together with a supply of silkworm eggs.

The life-cycle of the silk moth *Bombyx mori* begins with the eggs. These are the size of a pinhead and are kept in a cold, dry place until the temperature is right for hatching. After ten to fourteen days in the warm, a tiny caterpillar emerges and is set to feed on mulberry leaves. It has a voracious appetite and grows at an enormous speed, shedding its skin four times in the process, until it is from 3 to 4 in (8 to 10 cm) long. It then starts searching for a

08 place to spin its cocoon, at which stage some form of grid will be provided with just enough space for one worm, for if two inhabit one place and start spinning together the silk becomes impossible to reel. The worm, making a figure-of-eight movement with its head, produces a continuous filament of silk in liquid form emitted from two spinnerets, together with sericin, the whole hardening on contact with air. The worm meanwhile shrinks in size and changes into a

chrysalis, which in its turn emerges ten days later as a moth. But that happens only if it is allowed to complete its life cycle, for in fact the chrysalis is killed in the cocoon in order to prevent it breaking out and damaging the continuous filament of silk.

The chrysalises are stifled by being subjected to steam or heat, after which, in theory, they could be stored away indefinitely. However, in practice storage is not a good idea because not only do they take up a lot of space, but they are subject to attack from rats, mice, ants and mildew (Gaddum, 1979, p. 13).

The silk is first 'reeled' and then 'thrown'. To reel silk, the cocoons are placed in hot water in order to soften the sericin; then the ends of silk from about six to ten cocoons are gathered together, guided through wire or glass eyes and wound on to a reel. The resulting thread still appears to be single, as the extraordinarily fine filaments of silk dry as one when they are reeled together. During throwing, these single threads go through more winding, twisting and doubling processes, making a variety of silk threads from soft tram to tightly spun organzine.

A silk yarn is also made from spinning the floss which envelops the cocoons, together with other sources of waste silk. The silk at both the beginning and the end of the cocoon is not of the same quality as the silk that is reeled, and has to be put on one side; other cocoons may be damaged, spoilt, or not up to standard. All these sources of broken silk fibres are put together and spun in the same fashion as wool or cotton, making a soft rough thread referred to as 'spun' silk.

On the tiny island of Kume, 90 miles west of Okinawa, yet another method of silk spinning is practised. Each cocoon is opened up, turned inside out and stretched on a frame. Layer upon layer of fine silk (*mawata*) is stretched in this manner and then hung out to dry like a handkerchief. When dry, the *mawata* is fixed to nails projecting from a rotating stand, fluffed up and spun, making a soft weft thread to be used with the reeled warp. This method of spinning is fully described by Alison Mitchell (1985), who twice visited the island to learn and work with the villagers.

110 (above) Mawata *is prepared by opening each cocoon, turning it inside out and stretching it on a frame.*

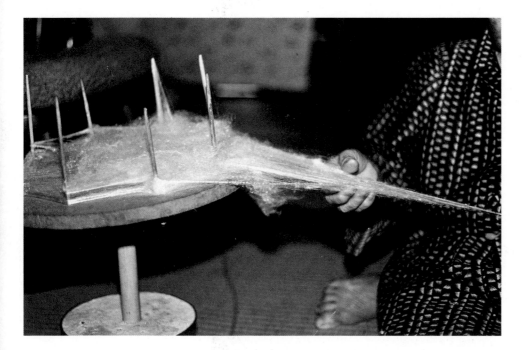

109 (facing page) *Many layers are superimposed before hanging the* mawata *out to dry.*

111 *The dry* mawata, *fixed to nails projecting from a turntable, are guided to the eyelet on a spinner (out of view on the right).*

Dyes

The colouring of *kasuri* textiles falls roughly into two groups: yellow through to brown, and blues. Occasionally spots of red, orange, green and purple make an appearance, but only in isolated examples. This preponderance of blues and browns is the result of using natural dyes that are easily available. The *kasuri* technique is a 'folk' craft, in the sense that it is often practised by women who also help in the fields: they are in no position to purchase expensive imported dyes when other sources of natural colour are all around them, albeit in a limited palette.

In Japan indigo, used for dyeing all shades from light to navy blue and referred to as *ai*, is obtained from different plants from those mentioned so far in this book. The most common one is dyer's knotweed (*Polygonum tinctorium*), an indigenous plant which is also cultivated. The leaves are picked before the plant has flowered, and are spread out on the floor under cover, sprinkled with water and left to ferment. After about eighty days the fermented leaves are pounded in a mortar and formed into indigo-balls which can be dried and stored. To prepare a dye bath, half an indigo-ball is dissolved in an alkaline solution to which is added lime, bran, soda ash and lye. The mixture is stirred and heated to 68°F (20°C), after which it is left to stand. In five to ten days bubbles start to form on the surface and more lime and bran are added to keep the solution alkaline. When it is ready for use the yarns are immersed and then hung out to oxidise. One dip is sufficient for a light blue, two or three are needed for a medium blue, and ten or more dippings are necessary for a navy blue. Each time the goods have to be aired for the same length of time as they are immersed in the dye bath (*Brooklyn Botanic Garden Record*, Vol. 20, 1982, no. 3).

Jun and Noriko Tomita (1982, p. 70) give detailed descriptions of dyeing with both natural and synthetic indigo. They specify *Polygonum tinctorium* and *Strobilanthes flaccidifolius* as the two indigo plants widely available to the common people, while Jill Goodwin (1982, p. 74) gives the oleander or rosebay (*Nerium tinctorium* or *Nerium oleander*) as the source of indigo in Japan. The oleander shrub is cut low like the silkworm mulberry to encourage the growth of leaves; these are picked in the summer. The indigo is extracted by a method of infusion, not the fermenting method previously described.

The touches of red or mauve, if introduced, can be obtained from the roots of *Rubia cordifolia*, one of the madder family, and the flowers of safflower, *Carthamus tinctorius*.

Yellows and browns are legion. The bark of alder and walnut and the wood of yew were some of the first dyes used by the Ainu to colour textiles. The bark of sumacs (*Rhus* species) and the Japanese chestnut (*Castanea crenata*) yield browns on their own, and brown/black with an iron mordant. The green outer coverings of walnuts are dried and stored ready for use for dark grey colours, a colour also produced by gall nuts. Yellows are obtained from the bark of the mountain cherry and *fukugi* trees, the leaves of the Japanese maple and the camellia (*C. japonica*), and the flowers of the pagoda tree (*Sophora japonica*).

No description of dyeing in Japan would be complete without reference to the water and mud which in certain parts of the country are rich in iron salts. 'There are some mineral springs at Arima, near Kobe in Japan, where the waters are so saturated with iron salts, that comparatively short immersion, and exposure to

112 *Dyer's knotweed* (Polygonum tinctorium).

air, will bring out a deep orange shade' (Pellew, 1928). In Kume the *tsmugi* silk is covered in mud containing iron, which changes the previously dyed yellow, reserved in the design areas, into rich browns for the background colour of their unique *kasuri* designs.

13

113 *Women taking a break from mudding. The silk skeins, spread out on the ground to the right of the picture, are caked in mud containing iron.*

The loom

For weaving country textiles in plain weave only a simple loom is used; nevertheless, a description of three different types is necessary to trace a development from the loom used in prehistoric times to the present day, although the introduction of a new loom did not mean the end of the old. The first is very simple and is still used by the Ainu; the second, the *jibata*, a low single-harness, body-tensioned loom; and the third, the *takahata*, a double-harness counter-balanced foot loom similar to the European loom and in fact distributed throughout the world.

THE AINU LOOM

Loom parts have been found which date the origins of the Ainu loom to about AD 100–200 (H. Pang, 1979). Yet Isabella Bird, in *Unbeaten Tracks in Japan*, published in 1880 (and recently republished in paperback), still came across women using it, as can be seen from the following description:

The loom is so simple that I almost fear to represent it as complicated by description. It consists of a stout hook fixed in the floor, to which the threads of the far end of the web [warp] are secured, a cord fastening the rear end to the waist of the worker, who supplies by dextrous rigidity, the necessary tension; a frame like a comb resting on the ankles, through which the threads pass, a hollow roll for keeping the upper and under threads separate, a spatula shaped shuttle of engraved wood, and a roller on which the cloth is rolled as it is made. The length of the web is fifteen feet, and the width of the cloth fifteen inches. It is woven with great regularity, and the knots of the thread are kept carefully on the under side. It is a very slow process, and a woman cannot do more than a foot a day. The weaver sits on the floor with the whole arrangement attached to her waist, and the loom, if such it may be called, on her ankles. It takes long practice before she can supply the necessary tension by spinal rigidity. As the work proceeds she drags herself almost imperceptibly nearer the hook. . . . It is the simplest and perhaps the most primitive form of hand-loom, and comb, shuttle, and roll, are easily fashioned with an ordinary knife.

From specimens of the loom found in museum collections and descriptions by Ling Roth in *Studies in Primitive Looms* one can fill in a few details which a Victorian traveller unacquainted with the mechanics of weaving might miss. One of the most interesting features is that a warp spacer lies between the far end of the warp attached to the post and the shedding devices, rather than between the shedding devices and the weaver, which is its more usual place. (This, incidentally, disposes of the need for laze rods to keep the warp threads in order.) Another interesting feature of the Ainu loom is that, although Isabella Bird describes a hollow roll used in separating the alternate threads (a device used on many simple looms), Ling Roth illustrates at least six different shedding devices used in conjunction with the usual heddle bar. This variety of unusual shedding devices suggests that the loom evolved in Japan over many years and was not an import from mainland Asia.

THE JIBATA

It is likely that the *jibata*, meaning 'low loom', did come from China (via Korea) as, according to Yoshita Yanagi, textile curator of the Japan Folk Craft Museum, the *jibata* has been used since AD 202–220. It can be described as a transitional loom because it is a cross between a body-tensioned loom, such as the Ainu or the Indonesian loom, and a one-harness loom. The weaver's back is still used to produce the tension on the warp threads, but there is now a contrivance by which a pull on a strap around the weaver's ankle results in the lifting of the heddle bar or harness to produce the counter-shed. When the weaver moves her foot away, the harness drops back to its original position and the natural shed is ready for the insertion of the weft.

The loom consists of two horizontal side pieces lying on the ground or tilted at a slight angle, supporting a seat at one end and two sets of posts, one pair shorter than the other, at the other end. The farthest pair of posts supports the pivoted over-head rocking device, which lifts the harness that is attached by cords to two tilt arms when the lever connected to the weaver's ankle is drawn down. They also support, halfway down the posts, the paddle-shaped warp beam on which the warp is wound. (The beam is described as paddle-shaped because the narrow

11

square-sectioned centre part, on which the warp is wound, broadens out into two flat pieces of wood on each side, preventing the layers of warp from slipping off the sides and providing a larger surface on the ends to brace against the uprights.)

The two separator bars, which divide the odd from the even warp threads, move up and down in slots provided in the shorter of the two posts. The threads from *under* the warp separator bar are the ones which are lifted up by the harness because they are threaded through heddle loops. The threads from *over* the warp separator bar remain stationary.

The weaver sits on the seat, her feet out in from of her and a cord attached to the projection from the rocking beam around one ankle. The cloth beam is held in position in front of her by cords at each end connected to a back support, which is either woven out of thread and old rags or fashioned out of thin wood. The reed, which is made of fine bamboo strips fixed in a frame, rides freely on the warp. The shuttle combines the functions of a spool and a sword, sometimes being as wide as the cloth, with one thick and one narrow edge to the blade, and in some instances containing space for a spool (Miller, 1977).

The *jibata* features prominently in nineteenth-century *ukiyo-e* woodblock prints in which the minutiae of everyday life were depicted, confirming that it was in general use at that time; but now, with a few exceptions, it has been supplanted by the *takahata*, the 'high loom'.

114 Jibata *loom. This is a simpler version of the one described on the opposite page. Japanese woodcut from* Ukiyo Hyakunin Onna, *1681. British Museum.*

THE TAKAHATA

The *takahata* resembles a traditional two-shaft floor loom with a raised bench, breast beam, warp beam, overhead swinging batten containing the reed, and two counter-balanced harnesses, all contained within a stout framework. The warp threads are threaded through the heddles on the two harness frames alternately, and these are attached by cords to two foot pedals which are depressed in turn to make the two sheds needed for plain weave. A small boat-shaped shuttle is used, containing a spool of thread, the swinging reed having taken the place of the sword to beat home the weft.

The draw-loom held an important position in China and Japan for the weaving of figured silks, but a description of this complicated apparatus is outside the scope of this book and in any case it played no part in the weaving of *kasuri*.

Kasuri

The patterns on *kasuri* fabrics are dyed on the thread before weaving; they are not the result of inlay, tapestry or any other technique. In describing these fabrics it is therefore necessary to concentrate on the preparatory work rather than the weaving itself.

The structure of the textile is always plain weave, and it is usually a balanced cloth (that is, the number of warp and weft threads to the inch is the same), although the design may be emphasised by weaving a warp- or weft-faced cloth for a warp or weft *kasuri* design respectively.

There are many different ways of resisting the dye on the threads to be woven, the most important of which is binding up the parts of the yarn which are to remain uncoloured. Other methods include:

a Clamping the yarn between a pair of identical boards out of which the design has been cut: where the two surfaces of the design press the yarn that lies between them the dye cannot reach.
b Weaving the material with a temporary coarse yarn and dyeing it, after which the temporary yarn is removed, leaving little white spots on the permanent yarn at the points of intersection where the dye could not penetrate. The fabric is then rewoven with a plain fine yarn, showing up the spotted effect.
c Applying dye by hand to parts of the warp or weft yarns.
d Laying all the warp threads for the full width of the fabric on a special printing board and block printing colour on to it before mounting it on the loom.
e Dip-dyeing the yarns in various colours.
f Tightly plaiting the yarn before dyeing, to produce random effects.

The principal method, binding the yarn prior to dyeing, is described below. The binding can be applied to the warp or weft yarns, or both, and each process, together with a special technique called 'picture' *kasuri*, will here be dealt with separately.

WARP BINDING

This is perhaps the simplest method of obtaining a resist-dyed pattern in a *kasuri* fabric. It lends itself to the creation of arrow and chevron designs because they run lengthwise in the cloth, in the direction of the warp.

The number and length of warp threads necessary are calculated and wound

115 *Girl weaving at a* takahata *loom. One of a series of prints by Katsukawa Shunsho. British Museum.*

116 *Transferring the pattern marks from the stick to the stretched-out warps in preparation for tying. The fukugi trees on either side of the woman have a special bark which produces a bright yellow dye.*

117 *Warp* kasuri.

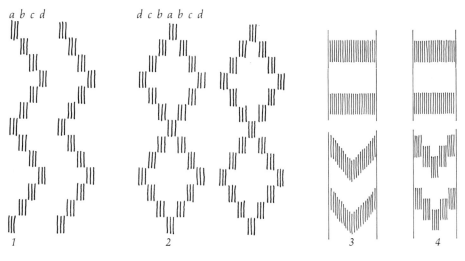

118 *Weft* kasuri.

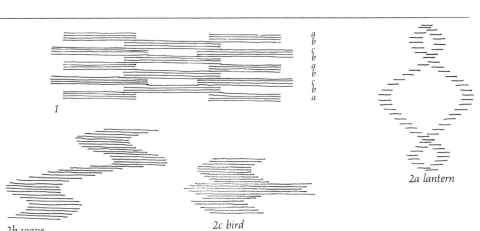

off, the warping posts often set up in the road where there is plenty of space and where help with the binding may be at hand. The resist areas in the design are marked on a stick and then transferred to the whole length of the warp. Fig. 117, no. 1 shows a very simple warp *kasuri* design of little bars meandering backwards and forwards. It is made up of four elements, marked a, b, c and d, which will repeat themselves across the width and length of the fabric. Sticks are prepared with the four parts of the design, and the requisite number of warp threads bound for each. A plain warp, the same colour as the background, will also be needed for the spaces between the meandering lines. When the warps have been dyed, rinsed and dried, the binding is carefully cut away and the four pattern warps and the plain warps arranged in the correct sequence in the raddle (a comb-like implement used for spacing the warp) preparatory to winding them on to the warp beam. The design in Fig. 117, no. 2 is woven with the same warps by rearranging the design elements.

The designs in Fig. 117, nos 3 and 4 might have had the design areas bound in horizontal bars right across the stretched-out warp threads, the correct distance apart, and then had them 'dislodged' into chevron shapes by shifting the position of small sections of the warp step by step when tying it on to the back beam. The Japanese have devised a 'warp-shifting box' as another means of doing this. The 'box' is put on the loom between the front beam and the harnesses. It is made of two rectangular boards which face each other across the width of the loom, secured the correct distance apart by bolted bars. The boards are punched with identical sets of holes. By threading rods through carefully selected pairs of holes and running different sections of the warp over different rods, a warp that has been dyed with horizontal bars will be 'shifted' into a predetermined design by the time the warp has been rolled onto the warp beam through the 'warp-shifting box' (Tomita, 1982, p. 61).

WEFT BINDING

Weft *kasuri* designs are woven on a plain-coloured warp. Skeins of weft are wound to a size just wider than the fabric to be woven, to make allowance for 'take-up', the extra length needed for the yarn to interlace the warp threads.

In the example illustrated in Fig. 118, no. 1, the resist areas of the design are made up by the arrangement of three different elements marked a, b and c. Therefore, for this design, skeins will be prepared with the three appropriately bound areas, together with plain dyed skeins for the areas in-between. After dyeing, drying and removing the binding material, yarn from the skeins is wound on to bobbins ready for weaving. As each different element making up the design is woven care must be taken that the resist area on the thread falls in the correct place.

Another method used in weft *kasuri*, illustrated in Fig. 118, no. 2a, requires only one small area of resist in the middle of the skein. The first row places this undyed area in the centre of the fabric, but in the second weft row it is pulled very slightly to the right, which throws the next undyed area slightly to the left and so on, these very slight adjustments producing diamonds or lantern shapes.

A third method, illustrated in Fig. 118, no. 2b, allows for greater freedom of design. Skeins of weft yarn are prepared which are considerably wider than the fabric to be woven, with one medium-sized resist area bound in the middle. In weaving with this yarn, each undyed area in the yarn is laid in exactly the position necessary to produce the motif representing water. The only undesirable side-effect is that it leaves loops of excess weft at either selvedge, which then have to be turned back into the next weft row. The bird, no. 2c, is produced in the same way but using two different skeins, the resist area for the body being slightly larger than that used for the wings.

PICTURE *KASURI*, COMPLEX WEFT BINDING

In addition to the foregoing simple designs, realistic motifs of fish, trees, animals and even buildings are produced with a technique called *e-gasuri*, or 'picture *kasuri*', invented by Taizo Otsuka of Kurume in 1839 (Tomita, 1981). The pictures have symbolic meaning and may combine two or more motifs such as 'crane-and-tortoise', symbols for longevity, or 'pine-bamboo-plum blossom', symbols for longevity, rectitude and harmony (Langewis, 1967).

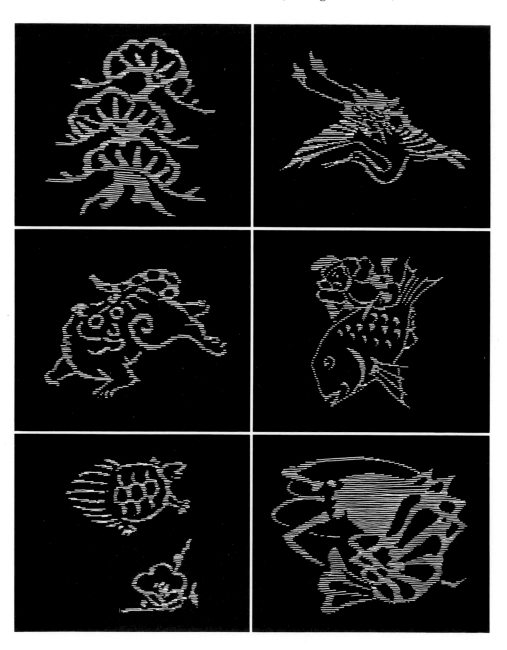

119 *Six popular motifs for* e-gasuri *(picture* kasuri*): (top) pine, crane; (centre) tiger, sea-bream; (bottom) tortoise and plum blossom, shrimp.*

120 Quilt cover with a repeating
design of an immortal riding a
carp, and a geometrical motif.
Fukuoka Prefecture, nineteenth
century.
London, Victoria and Albert
Museum.

The method requires infinite patience. First a drawing is made; then a board of the same proportions is prepared and two rows of fine nails are hammered in each side, spaced the exact distance apart so that when the guide thread is wound backwards and forwards across the board from one nail to the next, there will be as many rows to the inch on the board as there will be weft picks in the cloth. The drawing is placed underneath the guide thread and carefully transferred by waterproof pen to the thread. (Sometimes the design is printed on the thread with a wood-block.) The beginning and end of the first few rows are also marked, to help position the first few rows of weaving by aligning these marks at the selvedges.

The guide thread is then wound off the board and stretched out to its full length. As much weft yarn as will be needed for the length of cloth, which may be many repeats of the design, is stretched out alongside the guide thread, all the threads being bound together where the pen marks indicate. This is a long and laborious job, the endless knots of the binding being very tiring for the fingers. When binding is completed, the whole bundle is wound into a loose skein and dyed. After dyeing, and when the skein has been rinsed and dried and the binding material removed, the individual threads are isolated and wound into balls ready for winding on to the shuttle when needed for weaving.

The design can appear in four different ways according to whether the thread has been entered from the left- or right-hand selvedge and whether the yarn has been wound onto the shuttle from the beginning or the end of the thread. With the possibility of, say, a lobster appearing to the right or the left, or right-side-up or up-side-down, for example, many interesting pattern repeats can be devised.

COMBINED WARP AND WEFT *KASURI*

If the reader has understood the principles of warp and weft *kasuri* it will not be difficult to imagine where a combination of both techniques used together in the same fabric will lead. The method lends itself particularly to simple geometrical designs based on lines, stripes and squares, and can be found in the smallest designs – little crosses, known as 'mosquitoes' – to the big, bold rectangular designs based on the Japanese 'rice measure' or 'well pattern' design.

Horizontal and vertical shapes intercept each other, making strong designs in three tones; the intense dark blue of the background, pure white where the resist areas of warp and weft cross each other, and the 'half tones', to use a printing term, where the resist areas are only in the warp or the weft. The culmination of the art of *kasuri* must surely be when geometrical shapes are combined with *e-gasuri* figurative designs to produce textiles of simple perfection.

22

21

20

121 (facing page) *This recent textile by Jun Tomita clearly demonstrates the use of warp and weft* kasuri *in an abstract composition.*
Private collection.

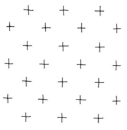

'mosquitoes'

rice measure or well pattern

122 *Combined warp and weft* kasuri.

6 SOUTH ASIA

Inlay weaving of Nepal

The independent kingdom of Nepal, full of beauty but one of the poorest countries in the world, extends for five hundred miles to east and west on the southern slopes of the Himalayas, bounded by Tibet in the north and India in the south. Geographically the country falls into three longitudinal regions: the narrow belt of low-lying land along the border with India, called the Terai, an extension of the Gangetic plains gradually rising into a low range of hills; the central range of mountains with high-lying valleys between 4,000 and 10,000 feet (1,200–3,000 m), which includes the Katmandu valley, the heart of Nepal; and the Himalayan ranges, 'the abode of snow', reaching to a peak of 29,000 feet (9,000 m), that form the border between Nepal and Tibet.

Owing partly to its geographical position, cut off by high mountains to the north and jungles to the south, and partly to its political situation, Nepal was virtually cut off from the rest of the world for more than a century. It was not until 1950, when the rule of the Ranas, the autocratic hereditary prime ministers, collapsed and the country was proclaimed a constitutional monarchy, that visitors and tourists were welcomed there. Two years later Mount Everest was conquered, capturing the imagination and bringing tantalising glimpses of this far-off country to the cinema and television screens of the world. Since then aerodromes, smaller airstrips and some roads have been built and tourism is growing apace, but it is still centred in the Katmandu valley, while the mountain valleys to the east and west remain comparatively isolated.

It is the weaving from the Koshi hills area in the east of Nepal that is the subject of this chapter, although other textiles are mentioned in more general terms. Mountain tracks connect the isolated villages, most of which are reached on foot, the only main road from India terminating at Basanthapur. In this setting, generations of Limbu and Rai women have woven fine *dhaka* cloth, a cotton textile with coloured inlay patterns used in the making of *topis* (the traditional men's head-wear), blouses and shawls.

In response to their need to earn more money than is possible by selling in local markets alone, the women have now, with the encouragement of KHARDEP (Koshi Hill Rural Development Scheme), developed the scope and variety of their weaving, building on their traditions. Formerly the *dhaka* cloth was woven in a limited colour scheme on a white ground, but now it is produced in exciting colours, sometimes using dark tones for the ground weave which give a luminous quality to the inlaid patterns. The sophistication of these new colour schemes and the inventiveness of the patterns have extended the market, even as far as Liberty's of Regent Street and the British Museum shop in London.

Plain, striped and checked cotton cloth is also woven by the Limbu and Rai women for their own use, and wool is woven by the Bhotes – the Sherpa, Tamang and Tibetan ethnic groups. Weavers among the Tibetans taking refuge in Nepal from the Chinese domination of their own country, and now the Nepalese themselves, also produce thick woollen pile rugs with Tibetan designs, sometimes executed in soft-coloured natural-dyed yarns.

123 New colour schemes and new uses for dhaka *cloth.*

124 *Cotton and acrylic topi, traditional headgear for men, from the Koshi hills.*

With the Tibetan border closed, wool is now in short supply; likewise, with the acute shortage of food, land can no longer be spared for growing cotton as it was in the past, so much of the raw material or yarn has to be imported. However, there is one source of fibre close at hand, for the nettle plant *Girardinia diversifolia* grows wild in great abundance in the northernmost district of the Koshi hills, and from the fibre obtained from it a yarn can be spun that closely resembles linen. The fibre, known as *allo*, has for generations been used for hard-wearing clothes, mats, sacks, porters' headbands and fishing nets. In response to requests by the people, KHARDEP has given practical help by improving methods of processing the fibre and suggesting new uses for it. Until recently *allo* had only been woven on back-strap looms in a plain warp-faced weave. Now successful trials have been made weaving *allo* in diamond and herringbone twills for cloth, which previously had only been woven in cotton. Cloth combining *allo* warps with woollen wefts, and finger-manipulated weaves for curtain and tableware are just two examples of goods which could have an appeal outside local or national markets, so important for bringing in much-needed money to the Rais, one of the poorest communities in this harsh environment.

Such industry as there is in Nepal, including jute and cotton mills, is situated in the narrow Terai belt on the Indian borders. The chief occupations in the rest of the country, excluding government employment or soldiering in the Gurkha regiments at home or abroad, centre round agriculture, portering and forestry. The establishment of cottage industries in the hill towns and crafts in the villages and homes could, by providing additional income to each family, help towards reversing the migration to the plains.

125 (facing page) *A sample of open-work (finger-manipulated weaves) in allo, for use as curtain material and tableware.*

Yarns

Wool, hair, *allo* and cotton are used in the Koshi hill area of Nepal. The wool used for blankets and clothing comes from the native Baruwal sheep. The fleece is short-stapled, strong and springy with good felting properties, and the sheep may be black, light brown or white, characteristics which are used to advantage in the thick blankets called *raris*. These are woven either in a balanced plain weave, or more usually a two-and-two twill, with an interlocking tapestry technique in which the black wool is used for the design and the white for the background. After being taken off the loom, the material is thoroughly felted by vigorous trampling with the feet on a smooth rock: this slightly obscures the design but considerably thickens the blanket.

The wool is cut from the sheep with a long, curved knife, then washed in baskets and teased out either by bowing, in the same way that cotton is bowed in other parts of the world, or carding with imported Indian carders. The wool is spun by the women either with hand spindles, resting the tip of the spindle in a bowl, or on the *charka*, a simple hand-operated spinning wheel similar to the one described in Chapter 4 on Indonesian textiles. Recently treadle spinning wheels have been introduced, increasing the rate of production.

There is an interesting description (Schmidt-Thome, 1975, p. 165) of a Sherpa method of spinning darning wool by hand (i.e., without the aid of a spindle). The wool appears to be teased out into a long, soft roving which is wound into a 'bracelet'. Several rounds are loosely twisted around the palm of the hand, making a very small skein which, in turn, is enclosed with a series of loops by chaining around its circumference. The 'bracelet' is worn on the left wrist and short amounts of the roving pulled out between the fingers and thumbs of both hands, twisting it into a thread and winding it on to a stick.

The Sherpa men also like to spin, especially in a sociable way, either while walking or while sitting on the flat roofs of their houses, which allows plenty of height for the spindle as it drops over the side! The men spin yak hair, using the spiked type of spindle with a wood or bamboo shaft and a pair of short wooden pieces crossed at right angles about two-thirds down the length of the shaft. The yak has coarse outer hair, which is used in rugs and bags, and soft inner hair, suitable for clothing or the lining of saddles, for example.

The *pashmina* goat also has two types of hair, the coarse outer hair used in rugs, sometimes together with yak hair, and the beautiful soft wool underneath used in the celebrated shawls from Kashmir. *Pashmina* is still used in the weaving of shawls, but only to a limited extent, as *pashmina* goats are rare in Nepal.

As already explained, *allo* is the local name for the huge nettle plant *Girardinia diversifolia*, which grows in profusion under the trees in the forest areas of Sankhuwasabha, high up in the north of the Koshi hill area and in other northern parts of Nepal. It is a tough, uncomfortable job harvesting the plants, as there are vicious stinging hairs on both the stems and leaves. Padded gloves help protect the hands while cutting down the plants and rubbing off the stinging thorns. The lower end of the cut stem is bitten into with the teeth, then the outer bark, which contains the valuable fibre, is stripped away from the inner stems, which are left to rot. The harvested bark is either subjected to a long boiling with wood ash, followed by rinsing, to remove the plant material and expose the fibres, or dried in bundles for use at a later date. Caustic soda, if it is available, helps in the

126 *Corner of a* rari, *a thick felted blanket woven in twill interlocking tapestry.*

127 (facing page) *Harvesting* allo: *the woman on the left is making an incision with her teeth in order to strip off the bark, as the woman in the background is doing.*

The art of the loom

extraction process by shortening the length of time needed for boiling the plant material — an important consideration when fuel is at such a premium.

The fibres from *allo* are among the longest in the world, strong and highly lustrous, but the production of the yarn is a long process. The fibres are boiled, neutralised with an acid (if caustic soda has been used), rinsed, scraped and rubbed with local clay containing traces of mica or even talcum powder, before being hung up to dry. When they are dry the spinner, sitting on the ground, stretches the bundle between her feet and her body, around her foot and underneath her left arm, so that with her free right hand she can gently pull the fibres apart. The fibre bundles are about 5 ft (150 cm) long; enough to twist around the spinner's waist as a neat and steady supply for spinning. A few fibres are eased out of the bundle and twisted into the yarn already on the spindle; the spindle is set rotating between thumb and forefinger and spinning now proceeds while either walking or sitting, every opportunity being given to this vital occupation.

As very little cotton is grown and spun in Nepal, commercially spun sewing cotton is imported from India and is on sale in the markets, as well as through branches of the Cottage Industries Emporium where the weavers take their finished products for sale. Commercial spinning and dyeing from cotton fibre, also imported from India, is now taking place in Dharan, producing a range of yarns for the weavers of *dhaka* cloth to choose from. Additional wool is imported from New Zealand to supplement the native Baruwal wool, although the Nepalese are in the process of improving and increasing all their livestock, including sheep.

Dyes

As has been mentioned earlier, the coloured yarn used for weaving the *dhaka* cloth in the Koshi hills area is mostly machine spun and pre-dyed. However, at workshops held recently in the hill villages, interest was shown in once again using some of the locally available plants for dyeing.

Munjeet (*Rubia cordifolia*) grows wild in Nepal and, with the addition of rhubarb, is used for dyeing reds and pinks. Called *majito* in Nepal, munjeet is a form of madder in which the whole plant is used and not just the roots as in the better known *Rubia tinctoria* and *R. peregrina*. Schmidt-Thome (1975, p. 176) gathered some interesting information on dyeing in his book on the culture and art of the Sherpas. He describes a plant called *tso*, which is almost certainly the wild madder plant, and, incidentally, the Tibetan word for 'colour'. This creeping plant, with stems as thick as a finger, is collected in winter when it is easier to find. By grasping the plant, the little roots can be carefully pulled out of the ground. The plants are then wound around the arm, rather as one would a rope, and taken home to dry by the fire or in the sun. The dried plant is best used powdered, rather than broken into little pieces, but this is heavy work and needs two people to take turns wielding the pestle, which is as thick as a man's arm. The chopped rhubarb which is used with it can be taken fresh, and the two ingredients are boiled with the material to be dyed. It is boiled for about an hour, after which it is left to stand over night before rinsing and drying.

The Sherpas use the leaves of a decidious tree called *chungen* for a yellow dye. The leaves are collected in the autumn, when the colour they give is at its best, and are either used straight away or dried for future use. They are stripped off the

branches and collected into bundles which are dried by the fire. At least once during this time the leaves are moved so that those in the centre of the bundle are brought to the outside and vice versa. Like madder, the leaves are powdered with pestle and mortar and mixed with the leaves and stems of a wild form of rhubarb. The yellow can be intensified with the addition of *pundok*, a raising agent similar to baking powder. The *pundok* alters the colour towards orange according to how much is used, but too much would be detrimental to the yarn.

The oxalic acid present in rhubarb is also used as a reducing agent when dyeing with indigo. The rhubarb juice is mixed with the indigo and left to ferment, thus reducing the indican which is insoluble in water to 'indigo white' (Denwood, 1974).

A black dye described by Schmidt-Thome (1975, p. 178) is made by immersing certain small nut-sized black stones in water and leaving them near a stove for several months, during which time they dissolve leaving a black liquid. This liquid is then combined with the powdered dried leaves of a plant called *tsapola*

Inlay weaving of Nepal   149

and a certain kind of salt obtained from India. The mixture is boiled for a long time before immersing the material, and then boiled again for a further hour.

Other natural ingredients used for dyeing are walnuts and onion skins, but how much all these different ingredients will be used in the future, when bright commercially dyed yarns are readily available, is difficult to tell.

The looms

Almost as many types of looms are used for weaving as fibres are used for spinning. The Bhotes in the north use three different types of loom for weaving wool and yak hair: the ground loom, a back-strap loom, and a horizontal frame loom with treadles.

The ground loom has been described in Chapter 2 on bedouin weaving: the warp is stretched between two parallel posts which are kept in position by four pegs stuck into the ground, two at each end. The Nepalese ground loom illustrated, however, combines the back-strap with the ground loom, the weaver's body providing the tension at one end and posts at the other.

Similarly, the Nepalese back-strap loom differs somewhat from that described in Chapter 4 on Indonesian weaving. In Nepal much longer continuous circular warps appear to be made, the beam farthest from the weaver being attached some distance away, such as to the lintel of the door, and sloping down at quite an angle to where the weaver sits.

129 *Body-tensioned loom. Shyio, Langtang valley.*

Inlay weaving of Nepal 151

The traditional Sherpa/Bhote loom is a two- or four-shaft frame loom with treadles, not dissimilar to a Western loom. It is made of wood and is portable as there are no fixed parts; all the parts are made in such a way that they slot into each other (no nails are used) so that it can be assembled or taken down with ease. This is essential, because the weaver often takes his loom to the house where the cloth is to be woven. It is about 36 in (90 cm) wide and 52 in (130 cm) from back to front, and the legs splay out at all four corners from the two horizontal side pieces through which the top ends project (see Fig. 7). These projections act rather as the pegs in the ground loom, keeping the back and front beams in position. The warp is wound on to the back beam and the cloth winds on to the front beam. The two pairs of uprights slotted into the side pieces and connected at the top support the two heddle bars from which the two pairs of harnesses hang. A cross piece connects the two side pieces underneath the heddle supports (not visible in the picture), and another cross piece between the front legs at ground level supports the four treadles. The weaver sits on a bench which is fixed to the legs of the loom. The ends of the treadles are attached by cords to the lower of the heddle bars, one to each, so that when the pedal is depressed the harness is lowered. For twill, two pedals are used at a time, one with each foot, lowering a pair of harnesses, the order dictated by the structure of the weave.

The treadle loom used in the Koshi hills has altogether a more fragile and temporary appearance. It may be made out of bamboo, or part wood and part

131 *Improvised loom of bamboo, wood and string: the warp-tensioning cord, attached to the upright of the cloth beam, is clearly visible to the right of the central weaver.*

bamboo – whichever is to hand at the time of making. The warp beam is placed some distance away from the weaver and hangs from a support made by two uprights and a cross bar. A pair of cross sticks are inserted into the warp when it is made and tied together tightly; the rest of the warp is rolled up together with bamboo sticks. These cross sticks, together with the wound-up warp, hang from cords over the cross bar and can be manipulated by remote control, because a tension cord attached to the cross sticks is tied low down to a post or upright part of the loom within easy reach of the weaver. Each time some cloth is woven and needs to be wound on the cloth beam, the tension cord is loosened to allow the cross sticks to come towards the weaver. When the cross sticks eventually get too close they have to be drawn through the warp to the far end again. Sometimes the cross sticks are dispensed with and the bundle of warp is tensioned around a post.

There are two or three pairs of uprights on the Koshi hill loom but no side supports. The two uprights nearest the weaver support the cloth beam; the next two uprights support the cross bar from which the heddle 'horses' hang (or 'birds' as the Nepalese call them); and the third pair of uprights or the single post, as already described, supports the warp. The reed/beater is attached by cords and also swings from the central cross bar. Cords connect from underneath the heddles to foot pedals, or with loops around the feet: the difference between crossing the left foot over the right, or the right foot over the left, is sufficient to raise and lower the heddles.

The three pairs of upright posts are semi-permanent fixtures in the ground and, indeed, may be used by more than one member of the family; but the cloth beam, reed, heddles, pedals and warp can all be dismounted, wound up and taken indoors at any stage during the weaving.

132 Workshop in Sankuwasabha. All the weavers are working on treadle looms, except the one sitting on the ground on the right, who is using a back-strap loom. The cross sticks and chained warp are in the centre of the picture.

Weaving

Before describing the weaving of *dhaka* cloth and its inlay designs, space should be given to the method of warping. The warp for a typical length of *dhaka* cloth, enough to make about forty *topis*, is 33 yds (30 m) long. (The woven *topi* lengths are cut off as they are needed and the warp retied on to the front beam: this length of cloth on the front beam would be virtually unmanageable.) Bamboo posts are set up in the ground in pairs, the two outside pairs 33 yds (30 m) apart, and another pair within that space 5½ yds (5 m) from the starting end (what will be the cloth beam end). The yarn is carried in spools on a stick so that they freely unwind, two or four at a time, and are guided around the posts, care being taken to separate and *individually* cross the threads at the pairs of posts in a figure-of-eight manner. When the warping is completed the crosses are securely tied, and in addition, two sticks are tied tightly into the one which was made 5½ yds (5 m) away from the starting point.

133 (facing page) Dhaka *cloth.*
The design elements take a diagonal path across the cloth.

134 *Contemplating the next move, a stranded embroidery thread in each hand.*

135 Dhaka *cloth scarf. Stranded cotton thread is used for the inlaid supplementary weft.*

In order to thread the warp through the reed, the beater holding the reed is placed on the ground between the weaver and her assistant. The weaver has the warp and the pair of warp sticks on her lap and the cross tie at the short end in her left hand. She takes each loop in turn and presents it to the helper, who is ready to catch it on a threading hook projecting through a space in the reed and draw it through. (This means that there are two warp threads through each dent of the reed.) The person with the threading hook collects all the loops on a stick as they are drawn through the reed, after which the stick is tied to the cloth beam.

Cords are attached to the pair of tightly tied cross sticks which were inserted 5½ yds (5 m) along the warp, and stretched over the support at the far end (together with the surplus warp) which forms the warp beam. The cord from the cross sticks is connected to the tension cord which, as previously described, is tied to the front of the loom so that the weaver can release the tension as the weaving proceeds.

After the loom has been dressed with the warp, the heddles are made around the alternate warp threads, one, three, five, and two, four, six, etc., in order to be able to lift up half the threads at a time to make the space through which the weft is passed. Not only are the loops made above the warp but the same threads are encircled from below, although, in order to do this, the warp is temporarily turned over. The specific way the Nepalese make the heddles, using a *pirsa* to keep all the loops the same size, is described in detail in *Weaving in Nepal* (Dunsmore, 1990, p. 13).

Unlike the Tibetan/Sherpa loom which has two pairs of heddles, necessary for weaving the twills and diamonds which characterise their wool weaving, the Koshi hills loom has only one pair. The foundation of the *dhaka* cloth is a simple tabby weave, woven in fine mercerised sewing cotton set at between forty and sixty ends per inch (sixteen to twenty-four per cm).

The intricate inlay patterns are woven with stranded embroidery thread, and are laid in with each row of the ground thread. As many as a dozen separate bobbins of embroidery thread may be used at the same time, spaced across the warp. After opening the shed and inserting the ground weave shuttle, but not taking it right through, the weaver lays in the various supplementary wefts, each put in from the same side as the ground weave and taken out at the designated place to rest on the surface. The shuttle is then taken right through the shed and the wefts collectively beaten into place by the reed in its batten. The next shed is opened and the procedure repeated.

If the inlay colour is not needed for a few rows it will then leave a little 'skip' of thread as it jumps from one position in the ground weave to the next where it is reinserted. These 'skips' give the fabric a right and a wrong side, the side facing up during weaving being the wrong side. However, many of the designs are woven in such a way that one motif leads into the next without the need to skip, as in the designs which proceed in a diagonal direction across the cloth. Even in these designs a tiny loop or 'turn' appears, but they are sometimes an attractive addition, in which case one could say there is no 'right' or 'wrong' face to the cloth.

There is another similar method of patterning which dispenses with the ground weft and only uses the coloured yarns. This produces an effect similar to tapestry, but with the difference that it is still more or less a balanced weave (not weft-faced as in true tapestry). Where the colours meet they have to be linked or dovetailed around common or adjacent warp threads; otherwise, where one colour turned back on meeting the adjacent coloured thread, a hole would appear. (This is not the case in true weft-faced tapestry, where the rows are so compacted that holes do not show up unless, as in kelims, there are vertical colour changes.) The inlay patterns, on the other hand, present no problems with vertical colour changes as the colour is supported by the ground weave. It is surely the simplicity of this technique that allows the Koshi hills weavers such freedom of design.

136 Old servilleta *from Chichicastenango or Nahuala. The double-headed eagles, cocks and horses with their riders are set between wide striped selvedges. London, Victoria and Albert Museum.*

7 CENTRAL AMERICA
Brocaded motifs from Guatemala

Guatemala straddles the isthmus of Central America, lying between the Caribbean Sea to the east and the Pacific to the south-west. To the west and north the country is bounded by Mexico, to the north-east by Belize, and to the south-east by Honduras and El Salvador. Sea, rivers and the lines of latitude and longitude have contributed to the present-day boundaries of Guatemala, which was the centre of the great Mayan civilisation that reached its climax about AD 300–900 (Bushnell, 1965, p. 8). Pure-blooded Indians make up almost half the present-day population and live mostly in the villages in the chain of mountains to the north and north-west. It is in these villages, still relatively isolated from the modern world, that the tradition of weaving colourful textiles on the back-strap loom persists to this day.

There is scant evidence to the part textiles played in the classic Maya periods, because actual fabrics have not survived as they have in Peru. The direct evidence that remains is in the form of spindle whorls found in the highlands, reinforced by ancient Mayan sculptural carvings, reliefs and figurines from the lowlands, which show various styles of richly decorated dress. A representation of Ixchel, goddess of the moon, weaving, medicine, and childbirth, from the Madrid codex, shows her weaving on a back-strap loom of the kind still in use today. The early Spanish missionaries, entering the country at the time of the Spanish Conquest in the first half of the sixteenth century, left written records of the Mayan way of life as they found it, and refer to their 'famed' textiles.

Although all the separate parts of the Guatemalan costume are richly decorated, it is the blouse, or *huipil*, that takes pride of place. In shape the *huipil* could not be more simple, for it is made of one, two or three rectangular pieces of cotton cloth sewn together, then folded in half, with space left for the head. As it varies in width, so it varies in length: it can be short, stopping just above the waist; a little bit longer, so that it can be tucked into a skirt; or mid-calf length and worn loose over the skirt, as in the special costumes worn by women in connection with religious festivals. On the medium-length and long *huipils* the sides are sometimes left unseamed, but usually they are partially sewn up, leaving a space at the top for the arms to go through.

The decoration, in the form of embroidery, or more usually brocading (the subject of this chapter), cover the *huipil* to various extents, from just the shoulders, to the shoulders plus separate motifs scattered over the front and back, to lines of brocading from shoulder to waist, all but obscuring the ground weave. The ground weave may be white, blue, red, or some other colour, either plain or striped. The stripes heighten the interest of the design even if, as sometimes happens, they consist only of carefully placed lines of contrasting colour on the selvedges.

37 The women's costume is completed with a skirt, a sash or belt, ribbons for the hair, and a *tutze*, an all-purpose cloth used for carrying babies or goods, or used folded on the head as a shade from the sun. Other cloths used are a shawl and 36 *servilletas*, similar to napkins: the former is larger and the latter smaller than the

tutze, but all are decorated in distinctive ways. The *huipil, tutze*, shawl, and *servilletas* are traditionally woven by women for their own family as individual pieces on the back-strap loom, but the skirt is cut from continuous yardage woven by men on foot looms.

The skirt material, which is on sale in the markets, may be in a plain colour but more often a combination of colours is used in one of the following ways: striped in the warp or weft or both, making a plaid design; or using resist-dyed '*ikat*' yarn which in Guatemala is called *jaspe*, a speciality of the village of Salcaja. Either the warp or the weft yarns, or both, are used for *jaspe* designs. Sometimes the area tied up to resist the dye is no more than a quarter of an inch in length on very narrow stripes and these are distributed between other plain coloured stripes to very lively effect. In other materials wider bands with more complex designs of *jaspe* cross each other in both warp and weft, giving an all-over effect. Yet others reserve the name of the place of origin in letters in the weft yarn, to be repeated at regular intervals.

137 *An Indian woman in San Juan Atitán market, wearing the* huipil *and belt; on her head she wears hair ribbons and a* tutze.

138 Jaspe *material from Totonicapan. The ikat technique using resist-dyed weft yarns has been used for both the repeating design motifs and the lettering. British Museum.*

Brocaded motifs from Guatemala 161

The skirt length varies according to the town or village the wearer comes from, as does the way in which it is worn and the way it is made up. In one or two towns the skirt material is wide enough for only one width to be needed, the length being sufficient to reach from waist to heels. This is simply wrapped around the lower half of the body and gathered in by a sash, which is wound several times round the waist. However, many skirts use yards of material, the length of the cloth forming the circumference of the skirt; that is, the width of the material forms the length of the skirt. If the material is narrow, two pieces are joined together selvedge to selvedge to give the required skirt length. This join is often accentuated by the *randa*, a wide but closely packed faggoting stitch worked in different sequences of colour from each side alternately, forming a slightly raised ridge crossing the seam, sometimes as much as 2 in (5 cm) wide. If the ends of the cloth are also joined to form a tube, this seam too is finished in a similar fashion so that the skirt exhibits the distinctive feature of an embroidered vertical and horizontal bar, both of which are carefully positioned by the wearer.

As the skirt is not sewn on to a waistband, the belt or sash is an important item of clothing, for it keeps both the *huipil* and skirt in position. It is difficult to believe that such a relatively small item of clothing can encompass such a variety of forms. It can vary from 1 to $5\frac{1}{2}$ yds (1 to 5m) in length and from $1\frac{1}{2}$ to 14 in (4 to 35 cm) in width. It may be made in cotton, wool or maguey, or any combination of these three and use simple or complex stripes, plain backgrounds covered with brocade or embroidery, or be entirely woven in tapestry weave. A full description of these techniques is not within the scope of this book and the reader is referred to more specialist works. Mary Atwater's *Byways in Handweaving* (1954) and *Guatemala Visited* (1965) feature many different belt and sash techniques, and Peter Collingwood's *Textile and Weaving Structures* (1987, p. 115) describes an unusual form of tapestry woven belt. The most comprehensive and detailed work on all Guatemalan textiles was written by Lila M. O'Neale in 1945, based on field research carried out during four and a half months in 1936. These and more recent books are listed in the bibliography.

The headdress consists of variations on the use of ribbons with different hairstyles, not the soft satin ribbons used in the West, although these also are sometimes used. The ribbons of Guatemala are more substantial, often tapestry woven in cotton or silk. Typical are the headbands woven by men on special ribbon looms at Totonicapan. They are produced for sale in other localities as well as their own, and may include the individual requirements of the particular community for whom they are being made. Some of these Totonicapan ribbons are 12 ft (3.5 m) long and just over 1 in (2.5 cm) wide, charmingly woven in silk tapestry depicting birds, rabbits, and geometric motifs for about 2 ft (60 cm) at each end, the rest being a plain red.

According to the village a woman comes from, she will either loosely twist and coil the ribbon round her head like a turban or carefully construct a kind of halo by winding the long ribbon round and round the head, each layer exactly on top of the preceding one. There are many other versions of headbands or ribbons, some woven by women on the traditional back-strap looms.

As must now be apparent, great differences exist in all these items, in size, style of decoration and method of wearing. This is because the towns and villages have all developed their own traditions, which have been passed down from one generation to another with little change. Indeed, it is possible to identify the village a woman comes from by the clothes she wears. Examples are the distinctive colouring of San Juan Sacatepeques, in the department of Guatemala, where animals and birds are brocaded over a ground weave of red banded with yellow and mauve; or Nebaj, where human figures, animals and birds, all more or less the same height, are tightly packed in against a white ground. However, exceptions can be pointed to, and generalisations are dangerous; a detailed account of subtleties and changes appears in *A Century of Change in Guatemalan Textiles* by Ann P. Rowe, the Western Hemisphere Curator of the Textile Museum in Washington DC.

The continuity in women's costume is not so evident in that of the men. Their greater mobility in search of work in the towns, or in the 1980s in the wake of guerrilla warfare against the repressive government of the time, has led to them abandoning their traditional costume for more practical Western clothes, reserving the former, also unique to each town and village, for ceremonial use. How long, one wonders, will the women and young girls in the highlands of Guatemala continue to wear *their* traditional costumes?

139 *Spinning cotton. The women usually sit down to spin with a bowl beside them in which to twirl the spindle.*

Brocaded motifs from Guatemala   163

Yarns

Although wool, maguey, silk, rayon and acrylics are all used in Guatemala, the majority of textiles are woven in cotton. Two native varieties of cotton are grown, *Gossypium hirsutum*, a white cotton, and *Gossypium mexicanum*, a brown cotton known as *cuyscate* or *ixaco* (Deuss, 1981, p. 59).

The white cotton, a cash crop, is grown and spun commercially but the brown cotton is rarer and usually hand-spun. Mazatenango, capital of the Suchitepequez department, is the commercial centre for coffee, sugar-cane and cotton, and cotton grows in the surrounding district between the Pacific coast and the mountains in the west. From there the goods are taken to the market towns and villages inland, either as raw cotton for hand-spinning, or, as is far more likely today, in the form of ready-spun singles yarn. This singles yarn can be used as it is for weft but is not strong enough for warp, and this is where the simple spindle may still be put to use, either in plying two singles yarns together or for strengthening the singles yarn by putting in more spin. This is done by attaching the end of the spun yarn to the spindle and rotating it until so many extra turns per inch or centimetre have been inserted into the yarn. Spindles are on sale in the markets, and Lila O'Neale's description of women choosing a spindle puts one in mind of the present-day choice of a biro, where there is usually a pad of paper nearby for trying it out. 'Indian women try out spindles displayed by the merchant on a piece of pottery conveniently placed nearby' (1945, p. 8).

The preparation of the cotton, where this still goes on at home, differs slightly from that described elsewhere. The women and children remove the pod and seeds from the cotton bolls by hand, at the same time opening up the bunched-up fibres so that they are more evenly distributed. After a basketful of cotton has been collected, it is spread out on an improvised pad and rhythmically beaten with two forked sticks until it forms first a rectangular lap, then, by further beating, a long strip which can be wound into a soft ball ready for spinning. The women usually sit down to spin with a pottery bowl beside them in which to twirl the spindle. When the spindle is set spinning, a certain amount of twist is collected between the point of the spindle and the hand that twists it, while the hand holding the cotton lap drafts the cotton fibres by extending away as far as it will reach. The spindle hand meanwhile lets the accumulated twist run up into the drafted fibres, converting them into a yarn. This length of yarn having been wound on to the shaft of the spindle, the whole cycle starts again.

Sheep's wool was not known in Guatemala until sheep were introduced into the country at the time of the Spanish Conquest. Wool is used in the making of outer garments as protection against the cold and in blankets. One of the wool centres is Momostenango and it was here that Mary Atwater saw two girls carding wool for spinning. She writes, 'Instead of making little rolls [rolags] as most of us have been taught to do, they put on the cards twice as much wool as we do and took it off in two flat sheets, the size of the cards' (1965, p. 11). It may be that there is a connection between the flat lap of cotton and the laps of wool: as the preparation of fibres for the spinning of cotton was established hundreds of years before wool was introduced, it could be assumed that the wool fibres also needed to be arranged in flat sheets ready for spinning. Wool spinning is done with a large free-hanging spindle from a standing position, or on a hand-turned spinning wheel of European origin.

Maguey is a vegetable fibre obtained from various species of the agave plant. The leaves of *Agave sisalana*, a variety of sisal hemp, are used for ropes, cords and the twine from which the back-strap and cords used with the back-strap loom are made. O'Neale describes the hive of activity connected with the maguey fibre around the shores of Lake Atitlan (1945, p. 20). The preparation is not unlike that of linen. The large flat leaves are pounded with wooden mallets, then left to soak for some days in shallow pools, after which they are scraped to remove all the pulp. The long triangular arrangement of fibres that is left is then washed again and hung out to dry, after which it is ready for twisting.

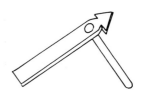

140 *A hand-held* maguey *spinner.*

Twisting, which resembles rope making, involves at least two people and needs space. Ends of the maguey fibre are attached to the short end of the twisting device, a stick handle protruding through one end of a tapering paddle which freely rotates with a circular movement of the wrist. The helper revolving the twisting device walks backwards away from the man feeding in the fibres for about 20 ft (6 m) while the cord is forming. It is then either doubled up on itself or left stretched out between pegs or nails while other cords are made with which to combine it. For plying, two rotating spinners are used, one in each hand.

Agave americana gives a finer, more elastic fibre known as *ixtle*, and is used by men in the making of bags for their own use. This may be spun by the thigh-spinning method. 'The spinner bares his thigh and rolls downward under his palm two small bunches of the fiber, which he keeps separated. When he considers that they have received sufficient twist he brings them upward under his palm, and in that one motion combines them in a twist of the opposite direction' (O'Neale, 1945, p. 20). However, Marilyn Anderson, a photographer who has made a special study of Guatemalan weaving, shows a photograph of a boy *leg*-spinning, and says that the spinning is not done on the thigh (1978, p. 43).

Silk, rayon, acrylics and softly spun cotton are used in decorating Guatemalan textiles. The imported silk floss is expensive and only used in ceremonial garments or for the *randas* on skirts. Rayon, which is an artificial silk made from regenerated cellulose, and acrylics are much cheaper and are therefore used extensively.

Dyes

Even before the arrival of chemical dyes at the end of the nineteenth century, strong bright colours were available. There was the whole range of blues from the indigo plant, reds (for dyeing wool) from the cochineal insect, purple from molluscs, and mauves, yellows, browns and black from various dye woods.

Indigo is the only natural dye to have continued in use in Guatemala into the twentieth century (Rowe, 1981, p. 24). Blues are a prominent feature in the *jaspe* skirt materials and one can still see the long warps stretched out by the side of the road with quite young children deftly tying up the areas to be resisted, often very small sections of about $\frac{3}{8}$ in (1 cm) repeated along the length of the yarn. After dyeing, the narrow stripes of resist-dyed yarns are interspersed with the plain coloured stripes when the warp is being assembled for beaming.

Anil (*Indigofera suffruticosa*), from which indigo is extracted in Central America, is reduced in a vat together with synthetic indigo, which is much cheaper, and the sacatinta plant (*Jacobinia spicifera*). Lila O'Neale writes:

The ground indigo, dye powder, and green leaves and stalks are put to steep in one of the vats. After a couple of weeks the dyer tells by the green colour on his stirring stick and the bubbles rising from the fermenting sacatinta at the bottom of the vat, by smell, and by the surface foam that the mixture has aged properly. The mass of greenish black foliage is dragged out, and the dye is ready for use (1945, p. 24).

The dye vat can be used for producing any shade from pale blue to dark navy, which they call black, depending on the amount of dippings (each dipping followed by oxidation in the air) and the strength of the dye bath.

Cochineal is no longer used commercially as a textile dye (although still used by natural dye enthusiasts), but it was of such importance historically as an export commodity that a little space should be given over to describing it. The colouring matter, carminic acid, is found in the body of the tiny cochineal insect, *Dactylopius coccus*, which lives on cacti: on the smooth leaves of the nopal, or the prickly leaves of the *Opuntia* group of cactus plants. The Spaniards, on discovering Central America, were excited by this new source for a red dye and started shipping large amounts of cochineal across the Atlantic. John Lloyd Stephens, an indefatigable traveller in the first half of the nineteenth century, wrote a detailed description of his visit to a nopal, or cochineal plantation in Antigua, the ancient capital of Guatemala:

. . . behind was his nopal, or cochineal plantation, one of the largest in the Antigua. The plant is a species of cactus, set out in rows like Indian corn, and, at the time I speak of, it was about four feet high. On every leaf was pinned with a thorn a piece of cane, in the hollow of which were 30 to 40 insects. These insects cannot move, but breed, and the young crawl out and fasten upon the leaf; when they have once fixed they never move; a light film gathers over them, and as they feed the leaves become mildewed and white. At the end of the dry season some of the leaves are cut off and hung up in a storehouse for seed, the insects are brushed off from the rest and dried in ovens, and are then sent abroad to minister to the luxuries and elegances of civilized life, and enliven with their bright colours the salons of London, Paris, and St. Louis in Missouri. The crop is valuable, but uncertain, as an early rain may destroy it; and sometimes all the workmen of a hacienda are taken away for soldiers at the moment when they are most needed for its culture. The situation was ravishingly beautiful, at the base and under the shade of the Volcano de Agua, and the view was bounded on all sides by mountains of perpetual green; the morning air was soft and balmy, but pure and refreshing. . . . I never saw a more beautiful spot on which man could desire to pass his allotted time on earth (1854, pp. 169–70).

O'Neale, writing a century later, describes the production of cochineal in the rainy season, when the fleshy leaves are tied in rows on light frames specially made for the purpose. On some of the leaves a few insects are attached, pinned on to the leaf in a small muslin bag. The insects lay their eggs through the muslin bag, and the bags are moved until all the leaves have eggs on them. The frames are left outside, leaning against the wall, but can presumably be brought under cover as soon as it starts to rain (O'Neale, 1945, p. 30).

When the eggs have hatched and the insects matured, they are brushed or shaken off the leaves into baskets and either killed in hot water and dried in the sun, or stove-dried straight away.

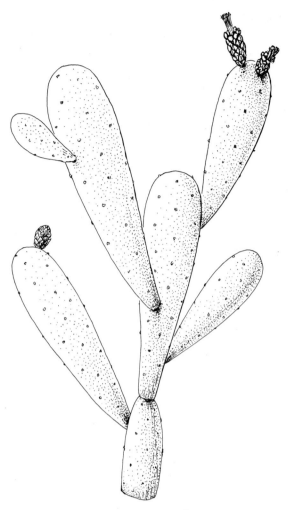

Cochineal's importance as an export commodity was not mirrored by its use at home since the dye's affinity is for wool and silk; cotton, which is the most used fibre in Guatemala, is not receptive to cochineal. The popularity of red as a colouring matter in textiles commenced with the introduction of alizarin (a coal-tar-based dye) patented in both Germany and England in 1871 (Carlsen and Wenger, p. 369).

Wood dyes also played an important part in trade with Europe. Logwood, the wood of the *Haematoxylon campechianum* tree, which was unknown in Europe before the discovery of America, is used for dyeing black, although lighter shades produce mauves. The heartwood of the tree is used for dyeing and is bought from the retailer in chips although it is transported as logs (hence its name). Dyeing is a simple matter as the dye runs quickly into the water, and the most important mordant used with it is copper salts. Other important wood dyes are fustic (*Chlorophora tinctoria*) for yellows, and brazil wood (*Caesalpinia echinata*) for reds, both mordanted with chrome.

The chemical dyes in use today have meant that the choice of colour available to the weaver is considerably larger than in the past; colours have been invented that never existed before, and this is reflected in the costume. Even so, red and blue still seem to be the dominant colours, and it is interesting to speculate whether this is a tradition left over from the time when alizarin and indigo were the two most popular dyes.

142 'The back-strap loom used exclusively by women. A lease stick, pattern sticks, shed rod, heddle rod and sword batten can be seen in position (starting from the top).

The looms

The back-strap loom is used exclusively by women, either in or outside their own house or in groups with other women. The tension of the warp threads is maintained between the weaver's body and a fixed point, making a far more responsive tool on which to weave than a rigidly built loom. A forward move of the body allows the weaver to lift the heddle bar or move the shed rod forward with ease, while leaning back tautens the warp threads, ready for the heavy throw of the sword when beating the weft in position. It is this instinctive rhythm backwards and forwards which is learnt from an early age.

Weaving is one of the many activities fitted into the working day, sometimes a companionable time with many looms stretched out from the same post or tree, and children and animals all round. The women of Guatemala used to weave mainly for themselves and their family, but now it has become a commercial necessity to weave for tourists, and many parts of the costume are made for sale.

The loom could be described as made up of a bunch of sticks and is, indeed, sometimes referred to as the stick-loom. It comprises two bars, one each at back and front, between which the warp is stretched, with lease stick, shed rod and heddle bar. The back bar is notched at each end and a rope attached, with which it can be hooked on to a post or branch at a convenient height so that it slants down to where the weaver kneels on the ground. The front bar, also notched, has the back-strap attached to it, sometimes woven in maguey yarn to make a comfortably shaped piece. Placed in the warp between these two bars, starting from the back, are a lease stick separating the odd from the even threads (for example, the even threads going over the lease stick), a shed rod under the odd-numbered warp threads, and a heddle rod with a continuous heddle enveloping the even-numbered warp threads by which it lifts them up. The weaver also needs a sword-like batten to keep the shed open and for beating down the weft, a stick bobbin on which the weft yarn is wound, a cloth bar for winding in together with the front bar when the cloth is wound on, a tenter-hook (a stick with a thorn embedded at each end and inserted underneath the web) for keeping the fabric the correct width, and additionally some small implements, thorns or sticks for picking up groups of warp threads when brocading.

143 *The warp being made to the required length on a warping board.*

145 (facing page) *Part of the central panel of a* huipil *from Chichicastenango. The two-faced brocading is raised between each warp thread to produce an uncut 'pile' effect. British Museum.*

144 *Weaving in San Antonio Aguas Calientes. Additional pattern rods are inserted behind the shed rod and the heddle bar.*

Since many of the pieces are woven to exactly the finished size, with a selvedge on all four edges, a warp is made of exactly the length needed (allowance being made for the 'take-up' in weaving) on a warping board. The pegs on the warping board are arranged in such a way that either a very short warp for a *servilleta* or a long warp for one of the sections of a *huipil* can be made. In either case, provision is made for the cross at each end (see Figs 6d and 143).

After the crosses have been secured and the warp taken off the warping board, the front and back bars are put in position through the loops at each end and tensioned out between the weaver and the fixed point from which she is working. The weaver sits back on her heels or with her feet out in front of her, from which position she can regulate the tension of the warp with the slightest movement backwards or forwards. Her first task is to arrange the warp threads in groups along the front and back bars to make sure that they are parallel and spread out to the width of the finished fabric. The front bar which is in position at this stage is

only a temporary one, so her second task is to bind the warp on to a permanent front bar. (These bars are usually sold in threes for this reason.) She lays the permanent bar on top of the warp threads nearest to her, secures a string to one notched end and runs the other end through the gap made by the temporary warp bar. After securing it to the other notched end, she starts binding the two together between the groups of warp threads; a procedure very similar to that of the Navaho, whose rugs are similar in that they have four selvedges and no cut ends to the warp. The temporary bar can then be removed and the permanent one slipped down into position: the loom has then to be turned around and the other end of the warp bound to the back bar. While the loom is in this position the continuous heddle for raising the even-numbered warp ends is put in and a heading strip woven. The heading strip is important for establishing the correct width of the fabric at both ends before beginning to weave. The loom is then turned round again for the second time to its original position, and the sword and shed-roll exchanged so that the shed roll is behind, and the sword in front of, the newly made heddle bar. The weaving can then proceed.

This is the back-strap loom at its simplest, but sometimes more pieces are used. Additional sticks may be threaded in and out of the odd-numbered warp threads 14 going over the shed bar, so that if the weaver, while brocading, wants to lift every alternate odd-numbered thread, i.e., 3, 7, 11, etc., she pulls this stick forward, inserts the batten, and turns it on edge to produce the brocading shed. Likewise, she may want one or more additional heddle bars so that the continuous heddle attached to it can lift up alternate even-numbered warp threads, for instance, or some other combination that the brocading design requires.

Although this is the principal loom used for the brocaded fabrics, mention should be made of several other types of loom, some of which are used only by men, and some by men or women. The European-type foot loom, introduced into the country by the Spaniards, is used for weaving woollen blankets and yardage of cotton skirt material. Some material with small brocaded motifs widely spaced on the ground fabric is also woven on the foot loom, to take advantage of the speed at which the ground weave can be woven compared with the back-strap loom, even if the laying-in of the brocaded motifs by hand slows things up.

More elaborate brocaded motifs can be woven on the draw loom, a foot loom that has, in addition to the two harnesses necessary for plain weave, from thirty to one hundred additional pattern harnesses operated in sequence by a draw-boy (or girl) who stands at the side of the loom where the draw cords hang down ready to pull them in order. As each cord is pulled down it raises a pattern harness threaded with the warps to be lifted on that row.

The importance of belts and ribbons in the costume of Guatemala has already been noted. These are woven on various types of loom. The simplest resembles in every way the back-strap loom, except that all the parts are only a few inches wide (8 to 15 cm). Men as well as women weave belts but may set them up in different ways. O'Neale (1945, p. 35) describes watching a man weaving a belt on 'such an assemblage of sticks', in which the warp was stretched out on two bars between a tree at one end and two stakes driven into the ground at the other. The weaver sat on a low chair and, when he came to the point in the weaving when he could no longer reach, he moved the chair forward, the bar of the chair forcing the warp down and under, 'at the same time making the warp unusually taut'.

The loom used by the professional ribbon weavers of Totonicapan combines the principles of both a foot-operated harness loom and a body-tensioning back-strap loom. It consists of a small stout table with a raised structure that supports four harnesses. These are attached to foot pedals which make them rise and fall through slits in the middle of the table. A warp spreader is permanently attached to the front of the table but there is no front or back beam and no batten, for in all other respects this resembles a body-tensioned loom. The long warp circulates from in front of the weaver through the spreader, through the heddles, round a hook attached to a post in the ground some distance away, back across the side of the table guided by a bent nail, and finally around a small bar slipped under the belt of the weaver and back to its starting point. The tapestry woven bands and other intricately patterned belts are woven on such a loom.

Weaving

Even in a discussion limited to the fabrics woven by women on the back-strap loom, thereby excluding woollen blankets, skirt materials and most of the belts and ribbons, the variety of techniques used in Guatemalan textiles, especially in brocading, almost defies description. However, before describing the methods of brocading, we must look at the fabric on which it is done, for this fabric, or ground weave, has an independent existence in that it would still be a complete fabric even if all the brocading was removed.

The simplest fabric, sometimes used in *huipils*, is a muslin, a fine cotton cloth with a more or less balanced weave of about thirty to forty ends and picks per inch (twelve to sixteen per cm). However, most of the fabric woven on the back-strap loom is of a heavier, warp-faced variety; the resultant cloth is more hard-wearing than the lighter, more open muslin cloth.

The yarn is rarely used singly as, even if it has been sized, it may not have the strength needed to withstand the tension associated with the warp on the back-strap loom. So the structure of the warp-faced fabric is of the basket weave variety. This means that the threads move in groups of two or three in both warp and weft, or two warps to three wefts, and other permutations. These variations are called extended plain weave because the threads still weave over and under each other as in tabby weave, but in groups rather than singly.

There are many simple ways to embellish the cloth, the most obvious of which is, perhaps, the introduction of coloured stripes. In a warp-faced fabric, stripes are included during warping. Many fabrics have a coloured ground with contrasting warp stripes; others have a white ground, but with carefully thought-out coloured selvedges, sometimes quite wide. These play an important part in the overall design, especially when, for example on a two-piece *huipil*, the two selvedges come together in the front of the garment.

Other than with colour, interest can be added to the plain cloth by using multiple wefts at intervals, causing ridges in the cloth, or by introducing designs or figures in which supplementary threads are inlaid into the same shed as the ground-weave weft. Even when the inlaid thread is in a contrasting colour, the effect is 'low-key' compared with the brocaded fabrics, as the supplementary thread is covered by the alternate warp threads which subdue the colour; but there is a characteristic outlining effect when each coloured weft is taken up ready to insert into the next row, leaving a little loop of clear colour.

146 Huipil *from Nebaj (detail).*
The distinctive 'lacing' technique is
used to depict birds, animals and
humans in brightly coloured
brocading yarns.
Krystyna Deuss Collection.

Brocaded motifs from Guatemala   175

The bold and colourful designs typical of Guatemalan textiles are woven using brocading techniques. This brocading is sometimes confused with embroidery, because both techniques produce large colourful areas of design on a plain background; but while embroidery is applied to the finished cloth with needle and thread after it has been removed from the loom, the brocading yarns are inserted row by row as the weaving progresses.

SINGLE-FACE BROCADING

In single-face brocading all, or nearly all, of the brocading weft appears on the face of the fabric. When all the brocading is on the face, and none of it shows on the reverse side, it is a sign that the brocading has been worked on an open shed; that is, on the threads lifted by the heddle rod or shed rod before passing the weft. The brocading weft is inserted with the fingers or a pick-up stick over and under the selected warps making the pattern, and beaten in place with the ground weave. Because the fabric is warp-faced, and the brocading is carried out on one set of warps only, when the shed is changed the floats are sandwiched between the two sets of warp threads, leaving nothing showing on the reverse side.

If nearly all the brocading is on the surface but flecks of colour appear on the reverse, other methods have been used. The brocading has been worked on a closed shed and the floats that are to form the design on the face of the fabric are tied down by one warp thread (or sometimes a pair) at each end. The binder, as it is called, may vary on every row, taking one step to the left or right, making a chevron for instance. Alternatively, it may be in the same place in each row, producing vertical lines; or may alternate in each row, the binder in the second row being mid-way between that in the first, producing a brickwork effect. But in every case, only the amount of brocading thread tied down by the binder appears on the reverse side.

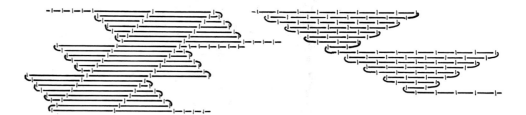

147 *Two examples of warp binders keeping the weft float in position.*

There are other examples of single-face brocading where the design is not tied down in a regular fashion, but which have large skips tied down in the middle in such a way that they produce what are called 'secondary warp patterns'.

The textiles from Nebaj are distinctive in both design and technique. The big, bold designs of figures, animals and birds are portrayed in a stylised manner with dense lines of colour following the simple shapes. These are worked in a single-face brocading by a means of 'lacing' the supplementary thread in a figure-of-eight fashion through a group of warp threads. In each row of brocading the coloured thread needed for each figure is taken, for example, over five, under three, back over three and under five, returning to the starting point. In the next row, when the shed has been changed, the brocading thread will repeat the same procedure, taking one step further to the left or right as the design dictates.

DOUBLE-FACED AND TWO-FACED BROCADING

In double-faced brocading supplementary wefts of different colours weave backwards and forwards, over and under groups of warp ends, appearing the same on the face and reverse of the cloth. This can be seen in the floral bands of *huipils* from San Antonio Aguas Calientes. The coloured wefts, used in translating the realistic designs found in embroidery patterns, are worked in and out over groups of four ends, covering the warp threads on both faces of the cloth as in tapestry.

In two-faced brocading, on the other hand, the face differs from the reverse. The supplementary weft also weaves in and out of groups of threads, either in geometrical patterns covering the width of the cloth (from selvedge to selvedge), or isolated motifs scattered over the field. However, in two-faced brocading the floats are of different lengths according to the design, and when the weft is not floating on the face of the cloth, it is floating on the reverse, resulting in a positive image on the face, and negative on the reverse. Irene Emery in her classic *The Primary Structures of Fabrics* (1994, pp. 164–6 and 171 ff) works her way through the minefield of definitions of terms used to describe textiles, the references to the particular matters touched on in this chapter being discussed on the pages cited.

In all brocading the sequence of steps is similar. The first shed is opened by drawing forward the shed rod, and the batten-sword inserted in a horizontal position in the space made. The weaver picks up the warp threads under which the brocading yarn is to go, either from the odd-numbered threads lying on top of the sword in single-face brocading, or from the warp threads lying in front of the sword in double-face. She lays in her brocading yarn, which may be one thread or many individual threads for the different colour areas spaced out across the row, and which is always thicker than the ground weft. The sword is turned on edge and the ground weft inserted, after which the two wefts together are beaten into position. The counter-shed, with the even-numbered warp threads, is then opened and the same procedure followed.

In describing the loom, mention was made of additional pattern sticks and heddles, and it is in brocading that these are used. Although the same designs can be woven without them, they save much time that would otherwise be spent counting threads, and consequently speed up the whole procedure. For example, where the same length skip is to be made in every row – for example, over nine threads and under one – the pattern stick would lie behind the shed bar under warps number 1, 11, 21, 31, etc. ready for use. Similarly, the pattern heddle would be prepared so that it picked up warps number 6, 16, 26, 36, etc. (half-way between the previous skips), the pattern stick and heddle being brought into play and used alternately when entering the brocading yarn. Remember that a row of tabby is woven with, or in between, every row of brocading. Three heddle bars and the shed roll can also be arranged to weave twills and goose-eye designs, as this is equivalent to the four shafts on a foot or table loom.

In spite of the possibilities of using devices to produce additional sheds, the majority of the designs do not lend themselves to these, and one is left full of wonder at the patience and skill of the women who painstakingly select a few threads at a time with fingers, a needle or a little stick, in order to insert their coloured thread, sometimes taking as long as six months to weave one *huipil*.

148 (facing page) Huipil *from San Antonio Aguas Calientes (detail), showing single and double brocading in the same piece.* British Museum.

149 (above) Huipil *from Chajul, neighbouring village to Nebaj (see Fig. 146). Detail showing the same 'lacing' effect.* Krystyna Deuss Collection.

150 Huipil *from Tecpan. Detail of brocaded motifs on a striped cotton ground.* British Museum.

Brocaded motifs from Guatemala   179

8 SOUTH AMERICA
Peruvian tapestry weaving

Textiles have played an important part in the Andean culture for several thousand years and it is fortunate for us that they have been preserved for posterity by a combination of two factors, each of which taken alone might have had different consequences. In the first place, textiles were held in great esteem, and for this reason were used to clothe the bodies of the dead – not only simple wrappings, but splendid sets of clothes were woven specially for the purpose and worn one on top of the other, the whole large bundle finally wrapped in a large and coarser cloth and placed securely in an underground grave. The second reason for the preservation of the textiles was the high saltpetre content of the dry sands of the desert where the graves were located (Anton, 1987, p. 9). If it were not for this set of circumstances, all the textiles might have perished without trace.

Peru is dominated by the Central Andes, the chain of mountains that follow the Pacific coastline of the South American continent. Between the coast and the highlands lies a narrow strip of desert traversed by mountain rivers draining into the sea. Communities established themselves at these points, where some cultivation was possible, but were separated from each other by the arid desert waste that lay between them. To the east of the mountains, inland, there are hot, humid slopes and tropical rain forests; but the area of excellence in textiles with which we are concerned lay in the highlands and on the coast.

For the purposes of discussion the country is divided into six parts, the highlands and the coast each being divided into northern, central and southern areas. Similarly, the immense time span covered by Peru's cultural history has been broken down into arbitrary periods by archaeologists, with Pre-ceramic (at least 2500 BC), Early, Middle, and Late Horizons separated by Initial, Early Intermediate, and Late Intermediate Periods, though the allocation of specific dates to any of these is subject to wide differences of opinion.

The Inca civilisation, in existence at the time of the Spanish Conquest in 1532 and well documented at the time, was the last in a long succession of cultures. It is only through the painstaking work of dedicated archaeologists, sifting through the evidence of the graves, that the different layers of successive cultures that preceded the Incas have been peeled back.

The earliest known textiles belonging to the Pre-ceramic Horizon, found in a valley off the northern Pacific coast, were made with maguey fibres and cotton and included a large proportion of twined textiles, some looping and netting, and only a small proportion of woven cloth of a coarse plain variety. Apart from traces of blue, indicating even at this early date a knowledge of indigo, the textiles were not dyed.

The highland culture of the Early Horizon centred on Chavin de Huantar in the north (approximately 1000 BC), the site of a temple and a place of religious pilgrimage. Stylised feline gods, snakes and birds appeared on the painted textiles, carvings and pottery of this period.

During the Early Intermediate Period, a time of technical evolution, the people produced the textiles found in the Paracas cemeteries on a narrow peninsula of the south coast. The cameloid fibres from the highlands, which for simplicity's sake will be referred to throughout as wool, had already been introduced to the coast and their affinity for natural dyes exploited to the full. Plain fabrics were now covered with fine imaginative embroidery in brilliant colours depicting human and animal forms. Cross-knit loop stitch used in decorative edges, complementary warps, and double cloths (the juxtaposition of two separate layers of contrasting coloured plain weave), are only three of the countless innovations of this period.

51

The development in the Paracas textiles was mirrored by the Nazca culture further south. To quote Junius Bird, writing of these two cultures in *Andean Culture History*,

In their totality, the textiles of Nazca and the Necropolis cultures present almost every weaving technique known in the Central Andes at any time. . . . In fact, the textiles of the South Coast represent one of the great artistic achievements of the Central Andes. The demonstrated skill in spinning, dyeing, and weaving techniques rank these textiles among the great arts of the world. The known quantity of woven fabrics is almost unbelievable (Bennett and Bird, 1949, pp. 172–3).

151 *Satin-stitch embroidery on a plain-weave background. Paracas (South Coast of Peru), c.200 BC–AD 100.*

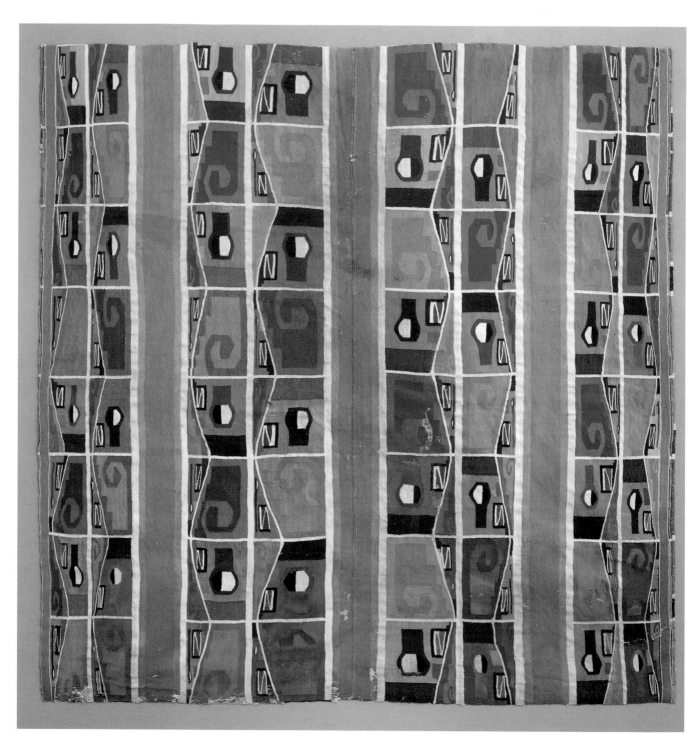

152 *Shirt from Huari, South Coast, c.AD 700–1000: interlocked tapestry with cotton warps and alpaca wefts. The bands contain characteristic Huari symbols: bisected disc eyes with tear pendant, composite N symbol, and a paired step-volute motif. James W. Reid Collection.*

The Middle Horizon, when the religious and cultural centres of Tiahuanaco and Huari had extensive influence, followed. Many features originating in Tiahuanaco, on the southern shores of Lake Titicaca, are found in Huari as well as other areas of south Peru and along the coast, where many examples of tapestry shirts and other textiles were preserved in the graves. They were woven with exceedingly fine wool, using a range of motifs that fall loosely into three groups.

The first group takes paired elements such as the stepped-volute and bisected eye with tear pendant, appearing together in a diagonally divided rectangular field; the second group consists of composite motifs combining several symbolic elements; and the third depicts staff-bearing figures, a design which may be hardly recognisable as over a period of time the process of abstraction moved a long way from the original (Sawyer, 1963).

The Inca, the last of the pre-Spanish great highland cultures, spread from the Cuzco valley over the whole of the country from Chile in the south to Ecuador in the north. More is known about this than any of the other cultures, because accounts of the Incas and their Spanish conquerors have been preserved in written records. The structure of society was based on a pyramid, with the Inca at the apex and the working peasants at the base. Rigid rules were enforced, dictating all aspects of everyday life including what clothes were to be worn and by whom they should be woven. For example, the Inca had four standardised treatments for their tapestry-woven tunics, the most striking of which were the chequerboard designs. It must have been dazzling to see the scarlet stepped triangle of the top portion of the shirt surrounded by black and white squares, the sides sewn together with colourful striped bands similar to the *randa* on Guatemalan skirts. A full account of the different styles of tunics can be found in *The Standardisation in Inca Tapestry Tunics* by John Howland Rowe (1979, pp. 239–64).

As tapestry is the subject of this chapter, it is worth considering the shirts and tunics of Tiahuanaco, Huari and the Incas in a little more detail. They were made from large rectangles with selvedges on all four sides, either one large one, or two narrow lengths of cloth joined together down the centre. In either case a space was left for the head, the rectangle folded in half at the shoulders, and the sides sewn together leaving spaces at the top for the arms. When the shirt was woven out of one piece, a slit had to be made in the centre for the neck opening. As many shirts were woven on their side (that is, the warp lay horizontally across the shirt when worn) the slit had to be formed of discontinuous warps, scaffolded over a thin temporary cord which was removed on completion.

The Incas' relatively brief reign, which had been run with clockwork efficiency, came to an abrupt end. The Spanish conquerors arrived on the scene at a time when the country was weakened by civil war. The supreme Inca, Huayna Capac, had recently died, leaving two rivals fighting for his position. The Spanish exploited the situation, causing the collapse of the empire.

Such a brief introduction to Peruvian textiles can do no more than hint at the long and complex history of the many cultures that produced them, any one of which could be the subject of a life-long study. Even if the centre from which a particular style evolved can be pinpointed, the influences, or dare one say fashions, stretched far and wide and cultural exchanges took place between coast and highlands, and between north and south.

153 *Standardised Inca shirt featuring tapestry-woven black and white squares and scarlet neck triangle.*

Fibres and spinning

The earliest fabrics found in Peru were made from plant fibres, such as maguey and cotton. It was the long-stapled cotton *Gossypium barbadense* that dominated the textiles found in the desert areas, having been cultivated since the third millennium BC. As well as white cotton, Peruvians are said to have at their disposal at least six distinct shades of naturally coloured cotton ranging from light tan through reddish brown to grey (Bennett and Bird, 1949, p. 259). Since cotton does not dye easily with natural dyes, except with indigo, this range of colours, contrasted with white, were used by the weavers in warp or weft stripes, ginghams and in pattern areas.

The spinner prepared the cotton by removing the seeds with her fingers rather than by ginning, in order to keep the arrangement of the fibres intact. This was not as tedious as it might sound, as a feature of this cotton was its absence of a fuzzy seed case. If the cotton was to be stored for future use, or dyed, this was done before removing the seeds. After the seeds were removed, the cotton was either attached to a forked stick (a primitive distaff) or teased out into a roving which could be coiled around the wrist.

Another practice was to beat the cotton in a similar way to that described in the chapter on Guatemala. The Peruvians, however, beat it into a large, flat shape resembling a pancake. It was then folded in half twice and rolled up tightly into a conical bundle, roughly 12 in long by 3.5 in (30 cm by 9 cm) in diameter at the base, and spirally bound with yarn. When needed for spinning, the cone was wedged into wooden supports stuck into the ground or tied to a post (Bird, 1979, p. 14).

The earliest surviving spindles have long since lost their shafts, only the whorls surviving. Nevertheless, hundreds of complete spindles have been found in graves of the Early Horizon and Intermediate Period, many found with cones of cotton in work baskets, buried with the weavers. The spindle was a long hardwood stick or thorn, about 12 in (30 cm) long, pointed at both ends, with a small painted ceramic whorl on the shaft. Nowadays, both well-made wood whorls or odds and ends, for example a bottle top or small potato, are used for extra weight on the shaft.

The spinner sat on the ground, rotating the spindle with one end supported in a bowl, leaving the hands free to draft the fibres. The fineness of the hand-spun cotton was quite remarkable, having a count of 250. (The count of cotton is based on how many hanks of 840 yd go to make up 1 lb; so a 250s count has 250×840 yd, which is 210,000 yd – very fine indeed.) Such a fine thread was strengthened either by giving it a hard twist when spinning, which produced a crepe yarn, or by plying.

Yarns are always plied in the opposite direction to which they are spun and this is usually done by rotating the spindle, when plying, in the opposite direction to that used for spinning. However, on the Peruvian north coast, the change is made by altering the postion of the spindle from vertical to horizontal, (across the spinner's lap), and in doing so moving the hand from one end of the shaft to the other. The spindle is still turned in the same direction, anti-clockwise in this case, but it has the effect of plying in the opposite direction (Vreeland, 1986, p. 370).

There are regional differences in both the direction of the spin and the

154 *Spindle/tapestry needle, yarn and two contrasting coloured cones of cotton with a fragment of tapesty, all from a work-basket found in a grave. British Museum.*

15

frequency with which single and plied yarns were used. This can be helpful in determining which geographical area a textile comes from. It appears that s-spinning and single ply more often appear on the north and central coast, whereas z-spinning and two-ply warps were those most frequently found on the south coast. The wefts used on the south coast in the Initial Period were single ply but by the end of the Early Horizon two-ply wefts were being used (Wallace, 1979, p. 45).

Whereas cotton is grown on the irrigated lands of the plains, wool is found in the mountains. The Peruvian wool comes from four species of the *Camelidae* family: the llama, the alpaca, the guanaco and the vicuna. The llama is important not so much for its wool, which is rated least valuable of the four, but because, like the camel, it is also a beast of burden, a source of food and a supplier of fuel. It can go for weeks without water, and is equally at home in the desert and the mountains.

Prescott, in his classic book *The Conquest of Peru*, describes the scene as found at the time of the conquest:

The flocks of llamas, or Peruvian sheep, were appropriated exclusively to the Sun and to the Inca. Their number was immense. They were scattered over the different provinces, chiefly in the colder regions of the country, where they were intrusted [sic] to the care of experienced shepherds, who conducted them to different pastures according to the change of season. . . . At the appointed season they were all sheared, and the wool was deposited in the public magazines. It was then dealt out to each family in such quantities as sufficed for its wants, and was consigned to the female part of the household, who were well instructed in the business of spinning and weaving. When this labour was accomplished, and the family was provided with a coarse but warm covering, suited to the cold climate of the mountains, — for, in the lower country, cotton, furnished in like manner by the crown, took the place, to a certain extent, of wool, — the people were required to labour for the Inca. (Prescott, [1847] 1963, p. 31).

155   The government also owned large flocks of alpaca, whose lustrous hair grows to nearly a yard in length, though the usual clip has a staple of about 9 to 10 in (23 to 25 cm). The colour range of white, black or grey as well as shades of brown and fawn make it a versatile fibre for weaving and knitting. Sir Titus Salt of Bradford was the first person in England to recognise the qualities of alpaca when he came across a sack of it in Liverpool and 'set himself to discover its capabilities. . . . The success of his experiments led to the erection of his great manufacturing establishment at Saltaire, in which 3000 hands are employed in the alpaca manufacture.' Imports of 560,800 lb yearly in 1840 rose to 3,878,739 lb in 1872 (*Encyclopaedia Britannica*, 1882, Vol. I, p. 596).

Unlike the llama and the alpaca, the guanaco and vicuna are undomesticated animals roaming high up in the mountains. During the Inca period they were rounded up at intervals by as many as fifty or sixty thousand men, and whereas some were slaughtered for their skins and meat, most were sheared and let loose again (Prescott, 1882, p. 89). The hair of both is a russet brown, fading off to fawn, but in addition the fibres of the vicuna are exceptionally fine and lustrous, sometimes likened to silk, and in the past the clip was reserved exclusively for the use of the Inca and his nobles.

Crossbreeding takes place between these four members of the *Camelidae*

155 *Alpaca near Huacahuasi, southern Andes.*

156 (left) *Woman spinning with a drop spindle, the fibres held on a forked stick. From the chronicle of Guaman Poma de Ayala.*

157 (right) *Upright loom depicted by Guaman Poma de Ayala in his chronicle.*

family and the names and a brief description of these different breeds appears in an article on the hair fibres in the *Journal for Weavers, Spinner & Dyers*, no. 132 (Seagroatt, 1984, pp. 18–19).

The wool yarn, like the cotton, was also exceptionally fine, often being no more than 0.5 mm in diameter. When used as weft it was rarely plied and was spun by the drop-spindle method associated with wool spinning. It is as familiar a sight now as it must have been thousands of years ago, to see women of both town and country spinning while going about their other business.

The availability of the two types of fibre, since almost a thousand years before Christ – cotton from the coast and wool (hair fibres) from the highlands – must have contributed to the early development of the tapestry technique, one that demands a strong, taut cotton warp and a soft, flexible woollen weft.

The looms

The loom used above all others in Peru is the back-strap loom, one that has already been described in some detail in the chapter on Guatemala. Not only is it used today, but there is ample evidence of its existence throughout this millennium. It is depicted on the rim of the Mochica pottery bowl illustrated, dated AD 600–1000, and many looms with work still on them have been found in graves of the same period. Centuries later, Guaman Poma de Ayala, who illustrated many scenes from the life of the Incas at the time of the Spanish Conquest, showed women weaving on a back-strap loom and a man working at an upright one, as well as women spinning.

But the back-strap and the upright were by no means the only types of loom, for the Peruvian Indians used a variety of devices for keeping the warp threads under tension. For example, Adele Cahlander (1985, p. 171) refers to many simple devices by letters of the alphabet: the A, V, X and U looms refer to very basic structures made from branches in the form of these letters, to which the two bars that tension the warp can be lashed.

The body itself can be used, as seen in the illustration opposite the title page: the end of the warp is secured by a string loop around the weaver's foot and the part of the belt she has already woven is tied around her waist, the tension being maintained between these two parts of her body. Very narrow warps are sometimes held taut between the left index finger and the big toe, or the loops of the two ends of the warp are slipped on to two sticks which are held apart by four posts stuck in the ground, two at each end. One must not forget that some of the warps were quite small, especially by Western standards, as each item was made independently, whether a pouch for coca leaves or a belt.

The width of fabric woven on the back-strap loom is limited by the reach of the weaver's arm while she holds the shuttle which is to be inserted between the two sets of threads of the warp, about 30 in (75 cm). There is no archaeological evidence as to how some of the very wide cloths were woven, but the ground loom (also called the four-stake loom), still in use, is one possibility. With a wide warp staked out on the ground it would be possible for several weavers to work side by side.

The tunics, which were 80 in (200 cm) wide, according to reports of the Spanish invaders, were probably woven on a loom made from four poles in the form of a frame and set leaning against a wall. Guaman Poma de Ayala illustrates

158 *Back-strap looms depicted on the side of a Mochica bowl, c.AD 600–1000. British Museum.*

159 (left) *Family group with a woman demonstrating the back-strap loom. Huacahuasi.*

160 (above) *Women in the village of Huacahuasi. One of them is spinning from prepared fibres worn like a bracelet on her left wrist.*

a man working at an upright loom. Two posts, branched at the top, support a cross beam to which the warp has been lashed, the other ends of the warp held under tension by another beam secured to the base of the two posts. Although the string heddle is clearly visible, no shed rod is indicated, although this does not necessarily mean none was used.

Another upright loom is depicted in a three-dimensional scene modelled on a jar found at Pachamac, described in one of the papers of the *Junius B. Bird Pre-Columbian Textile Conference* (Vanstan, 1979, pp. 233–8). It shows a loom with two thick uprights carefully hollowed out at the top to support the warp beam, with two warps attached to it one on either side. The two weavers are being supervised by a standing figure, but the little tableau is cut off at waist-height so it is not known how the warp is attached at ground level or whether the weavers are sitting in a kind of pit.

Perhaps the most interesting hypothesis concerning the creation of extra wide fabrics – and we are talking about cloth that is in rare cases 12ft (350 cm) wide – is that they were woven on a three-person back-strap loom. Truman Bailey constructed one from directions given him by one of the weavers who had seen or heard of such a loom from her mother. It is illustrated in *The Book of Looms* (Broudy, p. 80), but he does comment that it would be more suitable for tapestry weaving (where each person could work in small colour areas) than for a piece of cloth where the weft must travel from selvedge to selvedge.

The answer to how these very wide cloths were woven may not lie in discovering which loom was used, but rather which textile technique was employed. It would be quite possible to weave a triple cloth from a warp one-third of the finished size, the material opening up into three times that width when taken off the loom.

The dyes

The range of coloured yarns used, even in the earliest Peruvian textiles, those from the Paracas and Nazca cultures, is quite remarkable. O'Neale, comparing Paracas Necropolis dyed yarns with a coloured chart, distinguished 190 hues (Bird, 1949, p. 21), produced, however, not by that number of dyes, but by skilful mixing or top-dyeing of those available.

The three basic colours available were blue, red and yellow. The blue dye, indigo, was extracted from the leaves of *Indigofera suffruticosa*, and was used for all shades from a light sky blue to dark navy. Reds were obtained either from the cochineal insect growing on its host plants, the *opuntia* or *nopal* cacti, or from *Relbunium*, known in Quechua as *chchapi* (Donkin, 1977, p. 7). It has not been possible to identify the exact sources of the yellows on these ancient fabrics, but as many roots, barks, leaves and whole plants yield yellow, one can look to those plants still in use today. However, traces of the mordant alum have been found, confirming the early Indians' knowledge of this essential ingredient for fixing the colours on the yarn.

These three primary colours would have been used in various combinations by top-dyeing: for example, a quantity of wool first dyed to a medium shade of blue would then be dyed with yellow to make green, or with red to make purple.

It is important to remember that only a small percentage of the dyeing took place on white wool, and that the dye colours would have been substantially modified by the pigment already in the wool fibres. Yellow dyed on the grey alpaca wool, or blue on the light tan of the vicuna, would make olive or khaki shades. Dark tones of red and blue dyed on dark grey or nearly black wool would deepen the shades even more. Colours could be further deepened or modified by dipping the dyed skeins in mud containing iron, or by rinsing them in stale urine.

In spite of the extraordinary variety of colours found in the Paracas and Nazca textiles, those of later periods, for example from Chancay, Tiahuanaco, or from the Inca period, show a more restricted palette, whether through choice or circumstances prevailing at the time it is difficult to tell.

Inevitably, taking a leap in time to the latter part of the nineteenth and twentieth century, chemical dyes in powder form took the place of natural dyes. Kathleen McConnell, who studied plant dyeing with a Quechua Indian woman (1987, pp. 16–17) writes, 'Current plant dye techniques in Peru all seem to include an extra step; gather the plants, prepare them for dyeing, put them in a pot with enough water to cover, and then *aumentate de polvo* or "add dye powder".' Of course that was not the practice of her teacher, who tried to dye the way the Incas had in the past, as told her by her mother.

Fifteen years earlier, Barbara Mullins set out, with the encouragement of anthropologists, to try to find out what was used to make the dyes used in the ancient Peruvian textiles (1974, pp. 1825–7). Drawing on the information gathered from these two sources, one can fill in some of the gaps, assuming that the same plants might have been available thousands of years ago.

Mullins found that the most frequently used dye was walnut, a substantive dye; that is, it dyes without the aid of a mordant. Either the husks or leaves can be used, both of which produce brown. Yellow, the source of which is impossible to determine under laboratory conditions, could have come from the roots or bark of shrubs of the Barberry family; the leaves of a tropical bush called *tiri; rumiongo*, a moss growing on trees; or familiar onion skins. Soft reds might have come from *Coreopsis* or the fruit of the prickly pear (on which *Dactylopius coccus*, the cochineal insect, feeds).

All these plants, together with indigo, cochineal and *Relbunium*, the three important dyes already mentioned, provide a wide range of colours.

Tapestry weaving

Tapestry, when woven (for the word is sometimes mistakenly used for other forms of textiles), is the term used to describe a weft-faced fabric, usually depicting a design or picture with many separate wefts, one for each colour area, which together completely cover the warp. The designs of the Navaho rugs are woven in tapestry technique, as are kelims, but the term 'tapestry' is applied to wall hangings, which are lighter in weight, or to clothing, like that of the ancient Peruvians, which is still finer.

In a balanced plain weave, the space between each warp thread is the same as the diameter of the warp thread itself, but in tapestry the warp threads must be spaced slightly further apart, approximately twice the diameter of the weft thread, in order that the wefts can be compacted to cover the warps.

Having access to both cotton and wool, the Peruvians used strong, highly twisted cotton, either paired or plied, for the warp, and easily dyed, pliant wool for the weft. The weft is the active element that undulates over and under the taut

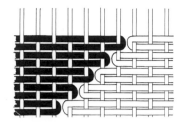

161 *Coloured weft moved one warp thread to the right on each successive pass. When the weft is compacted (not shown in the diagram), the angle is almost non-existent.*

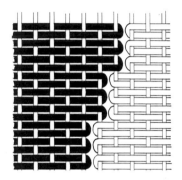

162 *An angle is built up with a series of small steps.*

163 *Pre-Conquest tapestry fragment, showing outlining of figure.*
British Museum.

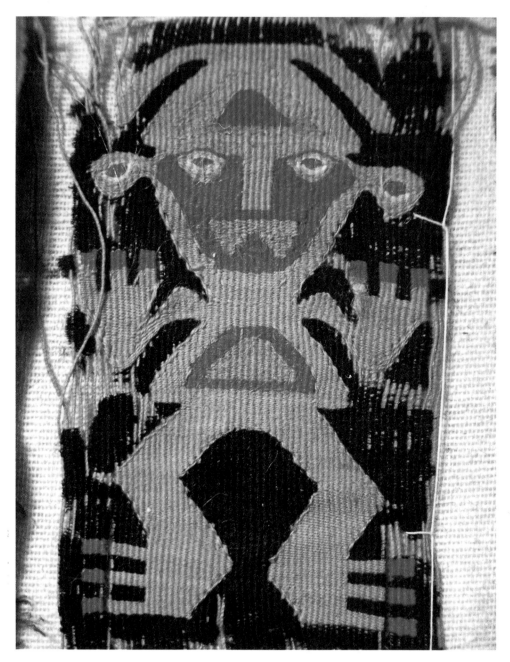

passive warps. The fineness of the yarns of both warps and wefts is astounding compared with Gobelins and other large tapestries woven for the dual purposes of decoration and insulation of draughty buildings.

D'Harcourt (1974, p. 23) quotes Crawford as examining a textile with 42 warp yarns and 260–280 weft yarns to the inch (16 and approximately 108 to the centimetre respectively), but between 20 and 30 warp yarns and 80 and 125 weft yarns to the inch (8 and 12 warp and 30 and 50 wefts to the centimetre) is more usual.

Although tapestry allows complete freedom of design compared with other techniques, it nevertheless presents several technical problems which have to be solved. Tapestries which are woven line by line, albeit with many different

coloured wefts, can only produce curved shapes by a series of different-sized steps. This is because the curve made at the meeting of two colours, if the colour is moved one warp thread to the right (or left) in each successive row, is so minute as to hardly count as a curve at all. A series of small steps, however, viewed from a distance, will look like a curve. If larger steps are made, to produce a steeper curve, a series of slits will appear at the boundary between the two colours, producing an effect also seen in kelims, of which they are a characteristic feature.

Small steps, not more than $\frac{1}{2}$ in (1.25 cm), are acceptable and do not weaken the fabric, but when the vertical colour changes become too deep, especially, for example, on the 3 in (7.5 cm) square checks of the Inca tunics, the length of the slits becomes unacceptable.

There are many different ways of avoiding slits when vertical colour changes are an integral part of the design:

1 *'Invisible' structural thread*
   A very fine weft is introduced into the fabric from selvedge to selvedge at regular intervals, holding the edges of the slits together. This is only possible when the weaving is proceeding row by row, which is not always the case, because it is sometimes more convenient in tapestry weaving to complete one motif of the design at a time. The illustration of weavers on the rim of the Mochica pottery bowl (Fig. 158) clearly shows this.

2 *Single interlocking between two warps*
   Two coloured wefts approaching from opposite directions in the same shed catch around each other in the space between two warps, before their return passage in the next shed. This makes a slightly fuzzy boundary between two colours.

3 *Double interlocking*
   The two coloured wefts interlock twice, both on the outward and return journey. This forms a ridge on the working side but a clear-cut boundary between the two colours on the reverse.

4 *Single dovetailing*
   The two coloured wefts turn around a common warp. This is suitable for short vertical colour changes, but has a tendency to build up into a hump over a greater length, distorting the horizontal alignment of the rows.

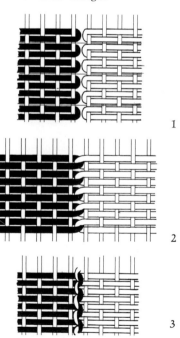

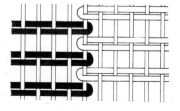

6

5 *Multiple dovetailing*
More successful is double, treble or quadruple dovetailing when two, three or four rows respectively turn around a common warp, the alternate groups of threads tending to compact into a wedge shape, each one dovetailing into the other, as the name suggests.

6 *Intermittent locking*
There are many examples where a relatively long slit is linked occasionally.

7 *Sewing*
Slits can be sewn up with a matching thread while weaving, or after the work has been taken off the loom. This can be done in a figure-of-eight stitch enveloping the two outside warp threads. Another way of joining the two sides of a slit, when the fabric is off the loom, is by catching the loops made by the return of the weft, alternately one from each side, and pulling the thread tight. This has the effect of introducing an extra warp linking the two colours together.

It has been assumed in the foregoing descriptions that the wefts lie at right angles to the warp, and that apparent curved areas of colour are in fact made up of horizontal and vertical colour changes of varying lengths. However, wefts themselves can curve, a style brought to perfection by the early Egyptian Copts, 164 but used less frequently by the Peruvians. A concave shape may be built up in the background colour by a series of small steps, as already described, and subsequently filled in by a different colour, the weft following the shape of the curve. Alternatively, a convex shape built up from rows of weft at right angles to the warp is subsequently covered by wefts following the contour of the shape.

Outlining, a popular device, is done in a similar way. Both geometrical and 163 curvilinear designs are frequently outlined, often in black. Two, three or four 166 rows of outlining weft are woven in plain weave: vertical outlines are either woven on two warps (the smallest possible unit) or a single warp is wrapped, in either case with occasional links to the colour areas on each side.

With a few exceptions, Peruvian tapestry weave has no right or wrong side, the ends of the yarn being hidden in the thickness of the cloth. The amazing skills of the tapestry weavers were not lost on the Spanish conquerors, and during the next three centuries fine tapestry continued to be woven, introducing European 167 figures, animals and Christian symbols. Tapestry weaving today cannot be compared with that of the past, and the expertise of the weaver of the twentieth century has been devoted to warp-patterning techniques.

166 *Outlining between coloured wefts.*

167 *Corner of a colonial tapestry, probably seventeenth century. British Museum.*

SOURCES AND FURTHER READING

Note
There are many references to the Swiss publication *CIBA Review*, an excellent source of information on all subjects relating to textiles. Where one specific article has been cited, page references are given. In other cases, all the articles in that particular number are of interest and no page numbers are given.

The Quarterly Journal of the Guilds of Weavers, Spinners and Dyers; The Weavers Journal; and *The Journal for Weavers, Spinners and Dyers* are variations in name over the years of the official quarterly publication of the Association of Guilds of Weavers, Spinners and Dyers of Great Britain.

INTRODUCTION

Looms and weaving
Albers, Anni, 1966, *On Weaving*.
    London: Studio Vista.
Baizerman, Suzanne, and Karen Searle, 1978, *Finishes in the Ethnic Tradition*.
    St Paul, Minnesota: Dos Tejedoras.
Beutlich, Tadek, [1967] 1982, *The Technique of Woven Tapestry*.
    London: B. T. Batsford.
Bird, Junius B., 1952, 'Before heddles were invented'.
    Handweaver and Craftsman 3(3).
Birrell, Verla, 1959, *The Textile Arts*.
    New York: Harper & Brothers.
Bridgewater, Alan and Gill, 1986, *Guide to Weaving*.
    London: Argus Books.
Broudy, Eric, 1979, *The Book of Looms: a History of the Handloom from Ancient Times to the Present*.
    London: Studio Vista.
Bühler, A., 1940, 'The essentials of handicrafts and the craft of weaving among primitive peoples'. *CIBA Review* 30.
Bühler, Kristin, 1948, 'Basic textile techniques'. *CIBA Review* 63.
Burnham, K. Dorothy, [1980] 1983, *A Textile Technology: Warp and Weft*.
    London: Routledge & Kegan Paul.
Collingwood, Peter, 1987, *Textile and Weaving Structures: a Source Book for Makers and Designers*.
    London: B. T. Batsford.
Crowfoot, G. M., 1941, 'The vertical loom in Palestine and Syria'. *Palestine Exploration Quarterly* (Oct.): 141–51.
Emery, Irene, [1980] 1994, *The Primary Structures of Fabrics*.
    London: Thames and Hudson.
———, and P. Fiske (eds), 1979, *Irene Emery Roundtable on Museum Textiles, 1977 Proceedings: Looms and their Products*.
    Washington DC: Textile Museum.
Forbes R. J., [1956] 1964, *Studies in Ancient Technology*, Vol. 4, 'Fibres, fabrics, washing, bleaching, fulling, felting, dyes and dyeing, spinning, sewing, basketry, weaving'.
    Leiden: E. J. Brill.
Gillow, John and Bryan Sentance, 1999, *World Textiles: a Visual Guide to Traditional Techniques*.
    London: Thames and Hudson.
Harris, Jennifer (ed), 1993, *5000 Years of Textiles*.
    London: British Museum Press.
Held, Shirley E., [1973] 1978, *Weaving: a Handbook of the Fiber Arts*.
    New York; London: Holt, Rinehart and Winston.
Horn, P., 1968, 'Textiles in Biblical times'. *CIBA Review* 1968/2.

Innes, R. A., [1959] 1977, *Non-European Looms: in the Collections at the Bankfield Museum Halifax*. Halifax: Calderdale Museums.
Roth, H. Ling, [1955] 1977, *Studies in Primitive Looms*.
    Reprint, Bedford: Ruth Bean.
———, [1951] 1978, *Ancient Egyptian and Greek Looms*.
    Reprint, Bedford: Ruth Bean.
Schaefer, G., 1938, 'The loom'. *CIBA Review* 16.
Seiler-Baldinger, Annemarie, 1979, *Classification of Textile Techniques*.
    Ahmedabad: Calico Museum of Textiles.
Sutton, Ann, Peter Collingwood, and Geraldine St Aubyn Hubbard, 1982. *The Craft of the Weaver: a Practical Guide to Spinning, Dyeing, and Weaving*.
    London: British Broadcasting Corporation.
Taber, Barbara, and Marilyn Anderson, 1975, *Backstrap weaving*.
    New York: Watson-Guptill Publications.
Thurstan, Violetta, 1934, *A Short History of Decorative Textiles and Tapestries*.
    Ditchling and London: Pepler and Sewell.

Fibres and spinning
Baines, Patricia, [1977] 1982, *Spinning Wheels: Spinners and Spinning*.
    London: B. T. Batsford.
Bally, W., 1952, 'Cotton'. *CIBA Review* 95.
Born, Wolfang, 1939, 'The spinning wheel'. *CIBA Review* 28.
Crowfoot, Grace M., and H. Ling Roth [1931] 1974, *Hand spinning and wool combing*.
    Reprint, Bedford: Ruth Bean.
Gaddum, P. W., [1948] 1979, *Silk*.
    Macclesfield: H. T. Gaddum.
Hochberg, Bette, [1977] 1980, *Handspindles*.
    Santa Cruz: B. Hochberg.
Hooper, Luther, 1919, *Silk: Its Production and Manufacture*.
    London: Pitman.
Kehren, M. 1956, 'The wool fibre'. *CIBA Review* 113.
Matthews, J. Merritt, [1904] 1924, *The Textile Fibers*.
    New York: John Wiley & Sons; London: Chapman & Hall.
Morton W. E., [1937] 1952, *Introduction to the Study of Spinning*.
    London: Longmans, Green.
Ross, Mabel, 1980, *The Essentials of Handspinning*.
    Malvern: M. Ross.
———, 1983, *The Essentials of Yarn Design*.
    Kinross: M. Ross.
———, 1988, *Encyclopedia of Handspinning*.
    London: B. T. Batsford.
Ryder, Michael L., 1968, 'The origin of spinning'.

Textile History 1(1): 73–82.
_____ , 1978, *Sheep and Wool for Handicraft Workers*.
Edinburgh: M. L. Ryder.
_____ , 1983, *Sheep and Man*.
London: Duckworth.
Schwarz, A., 1947, 'The reel'. *CIBA Review* 59.
Seagroatt, Margaret, 1984–6, 'Fibres'. *Weavers Journal* 130: 6–7;
Journal for Weavers, Spinners and Dyers 131: 11; 132: 18–20;
134: 7; 135: 20–1; 136: 18–19; 137: 13.
Varron, A., 1938, 'The early history of silk'. *CIBA Review* 11.

Dyes and dyeing
Adrosko, Rita J., [1968] 1971, *Natural Dyes in the United States*.
New York: Dover Publications.
Balfour-Paul, Jenny, 1998, *Indigo*.
London: British Museum Press.
Bolton, Eileen M. [1960] 1991, *Lichens for Vegetable Dying*.
Oregon, Robin & Russ.
Born, Wolfgang, 1937, 'Purple'. *CIBA Review* 4.
_____ , 1938, 'Scarlet'. *CIBA Review* 7.
Brooklyn Botanic Garden, [1964] 1982, *Dye Plants and Dyeing: a
Handbook*.
New York: Brooklyn Botanic Garden. A reprint of *Plants and
Gardens* 20(3).
_____ , [1973] 1978, *Natural Plant Dyeing: a Handbook*.
New York: Brooklyn Botanic Garden. A reprint of *Plants and
Gardens* 29(2).
Bühler, A., 1948, 'Dyeing among primitive people'.
CIBA Review 68.
Cannon, John and Margaret, 1994, *Dye Plants and Dyeing*.
London: The Royal Botanic Gardens, Kew.
Dean, Jenny, 1999, *Wild Colour: How to Grow, Prepare, and Use Natural
Plant Dyes*.
London: Mitchell Beazley.
Faber, G. A., 1938, 'Dyeing and tanning in Classical Antiquity'.
CIBA Review 9.
Gerber, Frederick H., 1978, *Cochineal and the Insect Dyes*.
Ormond Beach, Florida: F. H. Gerber.
_____ , 1978, *The Investigative Method of Natural Dyeing*.
Reprints from various US journals 1968–75.
Ormond Beach, Florida: F. H. Gerber.
Goodwin, Jill, 1982, *A Dyer's Manual*.
London: Pelham Books.
Grierson, Su, 1986, *The Colour Cauldron: the History and Use of Natural
Dyes in Scotland*.
Perth: S. Grierson.
Larsen, Jack Lenor, 1976, *The Dyer's Art: Ikat, Batik, Plangi*.
London and New York: Van Nostrand Reinhold.
Mairet, Ethel, [1916] 1946, *Vegetable Dyes*.
London: Faber & Faber.
Pellew, Charles E., 1928, *Dyes and Dyeing*.
New York: Robert M. McBride.
Ponting, K. G., 1978, 'Kermes and cochineal'. *Weavers Journal* 108:
12–17.
_____ , 1980, *A Dictionary of Dyes and Dyeing*.
London: Mills & Boon.
Robinson, Stuart, 1969, *A History of Dyed Textiles*.
London: Studio Vista.
Singer, C., 1948, *The Earliest Chemical Industry: the Alum Trade*.
London: Folio Society.
Thurstan, Violetta, 1957, *The Use of Vegetable Dyes for Beginners*.
Leicester: Dryad Press.
Wickens, Hetty, 1983, *Natural Dyes for Spinners and Weavers*.
London: B. T. Batsford.

THE NAVAHO

Amsden, Charles Avery, [1934] 1991, *Navaho Weaving; its Technic and
History*.
New York: Dover Publications.
Bennett, Ian (ed), 1978, *Rugs and Carpets of the World*.
London: Ferndale Editions.
Bennett, Noel, and Tiana Bighorse, [1971] 1977, *Working with the
Wool – How to Weave a Navaho Rug*.
Flagstaff: Northland Press.
Betterton, Shiela, 1991, *Navajo Weaving and Textiles of the American
Southwest*.
Bath: The American Museum in Bath.
Brough, S. G., 1988, 'Navajo lichen dyes'. *Lichenologist* 20 (3): 279–90.
Bryan, N. G., and S. Young, [1940] 1978, *Navajo Native Dyes: Their
Preparation and Use*.
Washington DC: Bureau of Indian Affairs.
Curtis, Edward Sherriff, 1907–30, *The North American Indian:
being a series of volumes picturing and describing the Indians
of the United States and Alaska*. 20 vols.
Seattle, Washington: E. S. Curtis; Cambridge, Mass: The University
Press.
Dockstader, Frederick J., 1978, *Weaving Arts of the North American
Indian*.
London and New York: James J. Kerry Ltd.
_____ , 1987, *The Song of the Loom: New Traditions in Navajo
Weaving*.
New York: Hudson Hills Press and Montclair Art Museum.
James, George Wharton, [1914] 1974, *Indian Blankets and Their
Makers*.
Reprint, New York: Dover Publications.
Kaufman, Alice and Christopher Selser, [1985] 1999, *Navaho Weaving:
1650 to the Present*.
San Francisco: Tulsa.
Kent, Kate Peck, 1961, *The Story of Navaho Weaving*.
Phoenix, Arizona: Heard Museum of Anthropology and Primitive
Art.
_____ , [1981] 1985a, 'From blanket to rug: the evolution of
Navajo weaving after 1880'. *Plateau* 52(4): 10–21.
_____ , 1985b, *Navajo Weaving: Three Centuries of Change*.
Santa Fe, New Mexico: School of American Research Press.
Latour, A., 1952, 'The textile arts of the North American Indians'.
CIBA Review, 90: 3247–54.
Pendleton, Mary, 1974, *Navajo and Hopi Weaving Techniques*.
London: Studio Vista.
Reichard, Gladys, 1936, *Navajo Shepherd and Weaver*.
New York: J. J. Augustin.
_____ , [1936] 1974, *Weaving a Navajo Blanket*.
Reprint, New York: Dover Publications.
Shuffrey, Margaret, 1988, 'The Navajo Indians and their rugs'.
Journal for Weavers, Spinners and Dyers 148: 12–13.

THE BEDOUIN

Balfour-Paul, Jenny, 1986, 'Indigo and south Arabia'.
Journal for Weavers, Spinners and Dyers 139: 12–19.
Bell, Gertrude, 1953, *Selected Letters of Gertrude Bell*.
Harmondsworth: Penguin Books.
Burkett, M. E., 1983, *The Last of the Bedouin in Jordan*.
Exhibition catalogue. Kendal, Cumbria: Abbot Hall Art Gallery.
Collingwood, Peter, 1956, 'An unusual method of handspinning'.
Quarterly Journal of the Guilds of Weavers, Spinners and Dyers 18:
608–9.
_____ , [1968] 1993, *The Technique of Rug Weaving*.
London: Faber.

——————, 1987, *Textile and Weaving Structures: a Source book for Makers and Designers*.
London: B. T. Batsford.

Crocker, Gigi, 1982, 'The traditional and current state of weaving in the country at large and in the pastoral community in particular'. The Sultanate of Oman: Part of UN project no. OMA/80/WOI.

——————, 1983, 'Omani weaving since the production of oil'.
The Weavers Journal 126: 17–20.

——————, 1986, 'Omani weaving in the 1980s'.
Journal for Weavers, Spinners and Dyers 140: 13–16.

——————, 1988, 'Traditional crafts: products and techniques'. *The Journal of Oman Studies Special Report no. 3. The Scientific results of the Royal Geographical Society's Oman Wahiba Sands Project 1985–1987*.
Muscat: Diwan of Royal Court Sultanate of Oman.

——————, 1989, *Traditional Spinning and Weaving in the Sultanate of Oman*.
Muscat: The Historical Association of Oman.

Crowfoot, Grace M., [1931] 1974, *Methods of Hand Spinning in Egypt and the Sudan*.
Reprinted, together with H. Ling Roth, 'Hand wool-combing', Bedford: Ruth Bean.

——————, 1941, 'The vertical loom in Palestine and Syria'.
Palestine Exploration Quarterly (Oct.): 141–51.

——————, 1943, 'Handicrafts in Palestine: primitive weaving. Plaiting and finger weaving'.
Palestine Exploration Quarterly (Oct.): 75–89.

——————, 1944, 'Handicrafts in Palestine. Jerusalem hammock cradles and Hebron rugs'.
Palestine Exploration Quarterly (Apr.): 121–30.

——————, 1945, 'The tent beautiful: a study of pattern weaving in Transjordan'.
Palestine Exploration Quarterly (Apr.): 34–47.

——————, and Louise Baldensperger, 1932, *From Cedar to Hyssop: a Study in the Folklore of Plants in Palestine*.
London: Sheldon Press.

Dalman, Gustaf Hermann, [1928–42] 1964, *Arbeit und Sitte in Palastina*. 7 vols (see vol. 5 for weaving and spinning).
Hildesheim: G. Olms.

Dickson, H. R. P., 1949, *The Arab of the Desert: a Glimpse into the Bedawin Life in Kuwait and Saudi Arabia*.
London: Allen and Unwin.

Faegre, Torvalid, 1979, *Tents: Architecture of the Nomads*.
London: John Murray.

Kay, Shirley, 1978, *The Bedouin*.
Newton Abbot: David & Charles.

Keohane, Alan, 1996, *Bedouin: Nomads of the Desert*.
London: Kyle Cathie.

Roth, H. Ling, [1951], 1978, *Ancient Egyptian and Greek Looms*.
Reprint 1978, Bedford: Ruth Bean.

Stanley, Martha, 1983, 'The bedouin saha weave and its double cloth cousin'. In *In Celebration of the Curious Mind. A Festschrift to Honour Anne Blinks on her 80th Birthday*.
Colorado: Interweave Press.

Thurstan, Violetta, 1934, *A Short History of Decorative Textiles and Tapestries*.
Ditchling and London: Pepler and Sewell.

——————, 1959, 'Bedouin life in the Libyan desert'. *Quarterly Journal of the Guilds of Weavers, Spinners and Dyers* 29: 6–10.

Weir, Shelagh, 1970, *Spinning and Weaving in Palestine*.
London: British Museum.

——————, [1976] 1990, *The Bedouin*.
London: British Museum Publications.

WEST AFRICAN NARROW-STRIP WEAVING

Adler, Peter and Nicholas Barnard, 1995, *African Majesty: the Textile Art of the Ashanti and Ewe*.
London: Thames and Hudson.

Austin, G., 1987, 'Nigerian handwoven cloth'.
Journal for Weavers, Spinners and Dyers 142: 15–17.

Boser-Sarivaxevanis, Renée, 1969, *Aperçus sur la teinture à l'indigo en Afrique Occidentale*.
Basle: Museum für Völkerkunde.

——————, 1972, *Textilhandwerk in West-Afrika*.
Basle: Museum für Völkerkunde.

——————, 1972, 'Les tissus de l'Afrique Occidentale'.
Basler Beitrage zur Ethnologie. Band 13.

——————, 1975, *Recherche sur l'histoire des textiles traditionnels tissus et teints de l'Afrique occidentale*.
Basle: Sonderabdruck aus den Verhandlungen der Naturforschenden Gesellschaft in Basel, Band 86.

——————, 1983, 'African textiles'.
Zurich: *Swissair Gazette* 11.

Bowdich, Thomas Edward, 1819, *Mission from Cape Coast Castle to Ashantee*.
London: Griffith & Farren.

Dupuis, Joseph, 1824, *Journal of a Residence in Ashantee*.
London: H. Colburn.

Eicher, Joanne Bubolz, 1976, *Nigerian Handcrafted Textiles*.
Nigeria: University of Ife Press.

Gilfoy, Peggy Stolz, 1987, *Patterns of Life: West African Strip-weaving Traditions*.
Washington, DC and London: Smithsonian Institution Press.

Johnson, Marion, 1980, 'Cloth as money: the cloth strip currencies of Africa'. *Textile History* 11: 193–202.

Kent, Kate Peck, 1971, *Introducing West African Cloth*.
Denver: Denver Museum of Natural History.

Lamb, Venice, 1975, *West African Weaving*.
London: Duckworth.

——————, and Judy Holmes, 1980, *Nigerian Weaving*.
Hertingfordbury, England: Roxford Books.

——————, and Alastair Lamb, 1973, *The Lamb Collection of West African Narrow Strip Weaving*.
Halifax: Bankfield Museum; Washington DC: Textile Museum (1975).

McLeod, M. D., 1981, *The Asante*.
London: British Museum Publications.

Menzle, Brigitte, 1972, *Textilien aus Westafrika*.
Berlin: Museum für Völkerkunde.

Picton, John, 1995, *The Art of African Textiles: Technology, Tradition and Lurex*.
London: Barbican Art Gallery in Association with Lund Humphries.

——————, and John Mack, [1979] 1989, *African Textiles: Looms, Weaving and Design*.
London: British Museum Publications.

Polakoff, Claire, 1982, *African Textiles and Dyeing Techniques*.
London: Routledge & Kegan Paul.

Rattray, R. S., 1923, *Ashanti*.
Oxford: Clarendon Press.

——————, 1927, *Religion and Art in Ashanti*.
Oxford: Clarendon Press.

Seiber, Roy, 1972, *African Textiles and Decorative Arts*.
New York: Museum of Modern Art.

Stanfield, N. F., 1969, 'Indigo dyeing in Western Nigeria'.
Quarterly Journal of the Guilds of Weavers, Spinners and Dyers 72: 1251–5.

——————, 1970, 'Spinning and weaving in Western Nigeria'.

Quarterly Journal of the Guilds of Weavers, Spinners and Dyers 73: 1288–92.
Teye, Alfred A., 1960, *The Traditional Kente Cloth.*
  Unpublished thesis. Kumasi: College of Technology.

INDONESIAN TEXTILES

Adams, Marie Jeanne, 1969, *System and Meaning in East Sumba Textile Design: a Study in Traditional Indonesian Art.*
  Southeast Asia Studies Cultural Report Series, no. 16.
  New Haven: Yale University Press.
————, [1965] 1999, *Decorative Arts of Sumba.*
  Holland: Peppin Press
————, 1972, 'Classic and eccentric elements in East Sumba textiles'.
  Bulletin of the Needle and Bobbin Club 55: 3–40.
Bolland, Rita, 1956, 'Weaving a Sumba woman's skirt'. In Galestin, Th. P., L. Langewis and Rita Bolland, *Lamak and Malat in Bali and a Sumba Loom*: 49–56.
  Amsterdam: Royal Tropical Institute.
————, 1971, 'A comparison between the looms used in Bali and Lombok for weaving sacred cloths.' *Tropical Man* 4, 171–82.
————, 1977, 'Weaving the pinatikan, a warp-patterned kain bentenan from North Celebes'. In Gerves, V. (ed), *Studies in Textiles History*, 1–17.
  Toronto: Royal Ontario Museum.
————, 1979, 'Demonstration of three looms'. In *Irene Emery Roundtable on Museum Textiles, 1977 Proceedings: Looms and their Products*: 69–75.
  Washingtom DC: Textile Museum.
Bühler, Alfred, 1941, 'Turkey red dyeing in South and South East Asia'. *CIBA Review* 39: 1423–6.
————, 1942, 'Ikats'. *CIBA Review* 44: 1586–611.
————, 1943, 'Materialien zur Kenntnis der Ikattechnik'. *Internationales Archiv für Ethnographie*, Supplement 43.
————, 1975/6, 'Patola'. In Bühler, Alfred, Urs Ramseyer and Nicole Ramseyer-Gypi, *Patola und Geringsing.*
  Basle: Museum für Völkerkunde und Schweizerisches Museum für Volkskunde.
Fischer, Joseph, *et al*, 1979, *Threads of Tradition: Textiles of Indonesia and Sarawak.* Exhibition held at the Lowe Museum of Anthropology, 1978–9.
  Oakland, California: University of California.
Fraser-Lu, Sylvia, 1988, *Handwoven Textiles of South East Asia.*
  Singapore and New York: Oxford University Press.
Gittinger, Mattiebelle, 1974, 'South Sumatran ship cloths'.
  Bulletin of the Needle and Bobbin Club 57.
————, 1979a, 'An introduction to the body-tension looms and simple frame looms of Southeast Asia'.
  In *Irene Emery Roundtable on Museum Textiles, 1977 Proceedings: Looms and their Products*: 54–68.
  Washington DC: Textile Museum.
————, [1979b] 1991, *Splendid Symbols: Textiles and Tradition in Indonesia.*
  Oxford University Press.
Haddon, Alfred C., and Laura E. Start, [1936] 1982, *Iban or Sea Dayak Fabrics.*
  Bedford: Ruth Bean.
Heinze (subsequently Dunsmore), Susi, 1969, *Art Teaching for Secondary Schools: a handbook of suggestions for teachers and students and all who are interested in the crafts.*
  Kuching: Borneo Literature Bureau.
Hitchcock, Michael, 1985, *Indonesian Textile Techniques.*
  Aylesbury: Shire Publications.

————, 1991, *Indonesian Textiles.*
  London: British Museum Publications.
Hose, Charles, and William McDougall, 1912, *The Pagan Tribes of Borneo.* 2 vols,
  London: Macmillan.
Jasper, J. E., and Mas Pirngadie, 1912, *De Weefkunst: De inlandsche kunstnijverheid in Nederlandsch Indie*, Vol. 2.
  The Hague: Mouton & Co.
Langewis, Laurens, and Frits A. Wagner, 1964, *Decorative Art in Indonesian Textiles.*
  Leigh-on-Sea: F. Lewis.
Morrison, Hedda, 1962, *Life in a Longhouse.*
  Kuching: Borneo Literature Bureau.
Raffles, Thomas Stamford, 1817, *The History of Java.*
  London: Black, Parbury and Allen.
Ramseyer, Urs, 1975/6, 'Geringsing'. In Bühler, Alfred, Urs Ramseyer and Nicole Ramseyer-Gypi, *Patola und Geringsing.*
  Basle: Museum für Völkerkunde und Schweizerisches Museum für Volkskunde.
————, 1984, *Clothing, Ritual and Society in Tenganan Pegĕringsingan (Bali).*
  Basle: Sonderabdruck aus den Verhandlungen der Naturforschenden Gesellschaft in Basel, Band 95.
Ross, Mabel, 1988, *Encyclopedia of Handspinning.*
  London: B. T. Batsford.
Roth, H. Ling, 1896, *The Natives of Sarawak and British North Borneo*, 2 vols.
  London: Truslove & Hanson.
————, [1955] 1977, *Studies in Primitive Looms.*
  Reprint, Bedford: Ruth Bean.
Solyom, Bronwen, and Garrett Solyom, 1973, *Textiles of the Indonesian Archipelago.*
  Honolulu: University Press of Hawaii.
Steinmann, Alfred, 1942, 'The patterning of ikats'.
  CIBA Review 44: 1612–18.
————, 1946, 'The ship of the dead in the textile art of Indonesia'.
  CIBA Review 52: 1885–96.
Wagner, A. R., [1959] 1962, *Indonesia: the Art of an Island Group.*
  London: Methuen.
Warming, Wanda, and Michael Gaworski, [1981] 1991, *The World of Indonesian Textiles.*
  London: Serindia Publications.

KASURI RESIST DYEING

Bird, Isabella L., [1880] 1984, *Unbeaten Tracks in Japan: an account of travels in the interior including visits to the aborigines of Yezo and the shrine of Nikko.*
  London: Virago.
Born, W., 1938, 'Weaving as depicted in Japanese art'.
  CIBA Review 18: 570-71.
Brett, K. B., and H. B. Burnham, 1965, *Japanese Country Textiles.*
  Catalogue of an exhibition at the Royal Ontario Museum.
  Toronto: University of Toronto Press.
Brooklyn Botanic Garden, [1964] 1982, *Dye Plants and Dyeing: a Handbook.*
  New York: Brooklyn Botanic Garden. A reprint of *Plants and Gardens* 20(3).
Goodwin, Jill, 1982, *A Dyer's Manual.*
  London: Pelham Books.
Gaddum, P. W., [1948] 1979, *Silk.*
  Macclesfield: H. T. Gaddum.
Hecht, Ann, 1982, 'Japanese textiles: with special reference to *kasuri* weaving'. *Weavers Journal* 122: 11–15.

Jackson, Anna, 1997, *Japanese Country Textiles*.
London: V&A Publications.
————, 2000, *Japanese Textiles in the Victoria and Albert Museum*.
London: V&A Publications.
Langewis, Jaap, 1960, 'Geometric patterns on Japanese ikats.
"Kultuurpatronen"'. Delft: Bulletin of the Ethnographical Museum 2.
————, 1963, 'Japanese ikat weefsels. "Kultuurpatronen"'.
Delft: Bulletin of the Ethnographical Museum 5 and 6.
————, 1967, 'Kasuri motif symbolism'. *CIBA Review* 1967/4.
Matthews, J. Merritt, [1904] 1924, *The Textile Fibers*.
New York: John Wiley & Sons; London: Chapman & Hall.
Miller, Dorothy, 1979, 'The jibata, a Japanese loom'.
In *Irene Emery Roundtable on Museum Textiles, 1977 Proceedings:
Looms and their Products*: 90–99.
Washington DC: Textile Museum.
Mitchell, Alison, 1984, 'Kumejima kasuri: weavers and dyers in
Kumejima'. *Weavers Journal* 130: 15–18.
————, 1985, 'Making silk in Kumejima'. *Weavers Journal*
135: 16–19.
Okamura, Kichiemon, and Kageo Muraoka, 1973, *Folk Art and Crafts
of Japan.*.
New York: Weatherhill; Tokyo: Heibonsha.
Pang, Hilda Dagodo, 1979, 'Loom representations in certain Ukiyo-E
woodblock prints'. In *Irene Emery Roundtable on Museum
Textiles, 1977 Proceedings; Looms and their Products*. 100–111.
Washington DC: Textile Museum.
Pellew, Charles E., 1928, *Dyes and Dyeing*.
New York: Robert M. McBride & Co.
Rathbun, William Jay (ed), 1993, *Beyond the Tanabata Bridge: Traditional
Japanese Textiles*.
London: Thames and Hudson.
Roth, H. Ling, [1955] 1977, *Studies in Primitive Looms*.
Reprint, Bedford: Ruth Bean.
Sugimura, Tsune, and Hisao Suzuki, 1973, *Living Crafts of Okinawa*.
New York: Weatherhill.
Textile Designs of Japan, 1964. 3 vols.
Osaka: Japan Colour Textile Design Centre.
Tomita, Jun, and Noriko Tomita, 1981, 'Picture kasuri: E-Gasuri –
a Japanese ikat technique'. *Weavers Journal* 119: 15–19.
————, 1982, *Japanese Ikat Weaving*.
London: Routledge & Kegan Paul.

INLAY WEAVING OF NEPAL

Campbell, A., 1836, 'Notes on the state of the arts of cotton,
spinning, printing and dyeing in Nepal'. *Journal of the
Asiatic Society of Bengal* 5: 219–27.
Chattopadhyay, K. P., 1923, 'An essay on the history of the Newar
culture'. *Journal and Proceedings, Asiatic Society of
Bengal* 19 (10): 465–560.
Collingwood, Peter, 1987, *Textile and Weaving Structures: a
Source Book for Makers and Designers*: 82, 86–7.
London: B. T. Batsford.
Denwood, P., 1974, *The Tibetan Carpet*.
Warminster: Aris & Phillips.
Dunsmore, Susi, [1983] 1990, *Weaving in Nepal: Dhaka-topi Cloth*.
Overseas Development Natural Resources Institute.
————, 1985, *The Nettle in Nepal: a Cottage Industry*.
Surbiton: Land Resources Development Centre.
————, 1988, 'Growing nettles in Nepal'. *Journal for
Weavers, Spinners and Dyers* 145: 9–10; 146: 17–18.
————, 1993, *Nepalese Textiles*.
London: British Museum Press.

Fürer-Haimendorf, Christoph von, 1975, *Himalayan Traders: Life in
Highland Nepal*.
London: John Murray.
Karan, Pradyumna P., 1960, *Nepal: a Cultural and Physical Geography*.
Lexington: University of Kentucky Press.
Schmidt-Thome, M., and T. Tsering, 1975, *Materielle Kultur und Kunst
der Sherpa*.
Innsbruck and Munich: Universitätsverlag Wagner.

BROCADED MOTIFS FROM GUATEMALA

Altman, Patricia B. and Caroline D. West, 1992, *Threads of Identity:
Maya Costume of the 1960s in Highland Guatemala*.
Los Angeles: Fowler Museum of Cultural History, University of
California.
Anderson, Marilyn, 1978, *Guatemalan Textiles Today*.
New York: Watson Guptill Publications.
Atwater, Mary Meigs, 1954, *Byways in Handweaving*.
New York: Macmillan.
————, [1946] 1965, *Guatemala Visited*.
Freeland, Washington: Shuttle Craft Guild Monograph 15.
Baizerman, Suzanne, and Karen Searle, [1976] 1980, *Latin American
Brocades: Explorations in Supplementary Weft Techniques*.
St Paul, Minnesota: Dos Tejedoras.
Bertrand, Regis and Danielle Magne, 1991, *The Textiles of Guatemala*.
London: Studio Editions.
Bird, Junius, 1953, 'Two Guatemalan wedding huipils'.
Bulletin of the Needle and Bobbin Club 37.
————, 1979, 'New World fabric production and the distribution
of the backstrap loom'. In *Irene Emery Roundtable on Museum
Textiles, 1977 Proceedings: Looms and their Products*: 115–26.
Washington DC: Textile Museum.
Bushnell, G. H. S., 1965, *Ancient Arts of the Americas*.
London: Thames and Hudson.
Carlsen, Robert S. and David A. Wenger, [1991] 1996, 'The dyes used
in Guatemalan textiles: a diachronic approach'. *Textile Traditions of
Mesoamerica and the Andes*, Margot Blume Schevill *et al* (eds):
359–78.
Austin: University of Texas.
Coe, Michael D., [1966] 1993, *The Maya*.
London: Thames and Hudson.
Collingwood, Peter, 1987, *Textile and Weaving Structures: a Source
Book for Makers and Designers*.
London: B. T. Batsford.
Deuss, Krystyna, 1981, *Indian Costumes from Guatemala*.
Commonwealth Institute exhibition catalogue.
London: K. Deuss.
————, 1996, 'A glimpse of Guatemala: a century of change in
Maya weavings'. *Ghereh: International Carpet and Textile Review* 10:
25–35.
Torino: CATO Editore.
Dietrich, Mary G., 1979, *Guatemalan Costume: the Heard Museum
Collection*. Exhibition catalogue.
Phoenix, Arizona: Heard Museum of Anthroplogy and Primitive
Art.
Emery, Irene, 1980. *The Primary Structures of Fabrics*.
Washington DC: Textile Museum.
O'Neale, Lila Morris, 1945, *Textiles of Highland Guatemala*.
Washington DC: Carnegie Institution of Washington.
Osborne, Lilly de Jongh, 1935, *Guatemalan Textiles*.
New Orleans: Tulane University.
————, [1965] 1975, *Indian Crafts of Guatemala and El Salvador*.
Norman, Oklahoma: University of Oklahoma Press.

Pang, Hilda Delgado, n.d., *Guatemalan Ethnographic Textiles: Background Data and State of the Art*.
  Bloomington: Indiana State University.
Pettersen, Carmen L., 1976, *Maya of Guatemala*.
  Guatemala City: Ixchel Textile Museum.
Rowe, Ann Pollard, 1981, *A Century of Change in Guatemalan Textiles*.
  New York: Center for Inter-American Relations.
Schevill, Margot Blum, 1993, *Maya Textiles of Guatemala: The Gustavus A. Eisen Collection, 1902*.
  Austin: University of Texas.
———— (ed), 1997, *The Maya Textile Tradition*.
  New York: Harry N. Abrams.
Sperlich, Norbert, and Elizabeth Sperlich, 1980, *Guatemalan Backstrap Weaving*.
  Norman, Oklahoma: University of Oklahoma Press.
Start, Laura E., [1948] 1963, *The McDougall Collection of Indian Textiles from Guatemala and Mexico*.
  Pitt Rivers Museum, Occasional Papers on Technology, 2.
  Oxford: Oxford University Press.
Stephens, John L., [1841] 1969, *Incidents of Travel in Central America, Chiapas and Yucatan*.
  New York: Dover Publications.
Wood, Josephine, and Lilly de Jongh Osborne, 1966, *Indian Costumes of Guatemala*.
  Graz: Akademische Druck.

PERUVIAN TAPESTRY WEAVING

Anton, Ferdinand, 1987, *Ancient Peruvian Textiles*.
  London: Thames and Hudson.
Bennett, Wendell C., and Junius B. Bird, [1949] 1960, *Andean Culture History*.
  New York: American Museum of Natural History.
Bird, Junius B., 1979, 'Fibres and spinning procedures in the Andean area'. In *Junius B. Bird Pre-Columbian Textile Conference*: 13–17.
  Washington DC: Textile Museum.
————, 1979, 'New World fabric production and the distribution of the backstrap loom'. In *Irene Emery Roundtable on Museum Textiles, 1977 proceedings: Looms and their Products*: 115–26.
  Washington DC: Textile Museum.
————, and Joy Mahler, 1951–2, 'America's oldest cotton fabrics'. *American fabrics* 20: 73–9.
————, and Louisa Bellinger, 1954, *Paracas Fabrics and Nazca Needlework: 3rd Century B.C. – 3rd century A.D.*
  Washington DC: National Publishing Co.
Bühler-Oppenheim, Kristin and Alfred, 1948, *Die Textiliensammlung Fritz Ikle-Huber im Museum für Völkerunde und Schweizerischen Museum für Volkskunde, Basel*. Denkschriften der Schweizerischen Naturforschenden Gesellschaft, Band 78, Abh. 2.
Bushnell, G. H. S., 1965, *Ancient Arts of the Americas*.
  London: Thames and Hudson.
Cahlander, Adele, with Suzanne Baizerman, 1985, *Double-woven Treasures from Old Peru*.
  St Paul, Minnesota: Dos Tejedoras.
Crawford, M. D. C., 1915–16, 'Peruvian fabrics'. *Anthropology Papers of the American Museum of Natural History* 12 (3 and 4).
————, 1924, *The Heritage of Cotton: the Fibre of Two Worlds and Many Ages*.
  New York and London: G. P. Putnam's Sons.
D'Harcourt, Raoul, 1960, 'Peruvian textile techniques'. *CIBA Review* 136: 2–40.

————, [1962] 1974, *Textiles of Ancient Peru and their Techniques*.
  Seattle and London: University of Washington Press.
Donkin, R. A., 1977, *Spanish Red: an Ethnogeographical Study of Cochineal and the Opuntia Cactus*.
  Philadelphia: Transactions of the American Philosophical Society 67(5).
Dwyer, Edward B., 1979, 'Early Horizon tapestry from South Coastal Peru'. In *Junius B. Bird Pre-Columbian Textile Conference*: 61–82.
  Washington DC: Textile Museum.
Feltham, Jane, 1989, *Peruvian Textiles*.
  Aylesbury: Shire Publications.
Fester, G. A., 1954, 'Some dyes of an ancient South American civilization'. *Dyestuffs* 40(9): 238–44.
Lothrop, S. K., 1957, *Pre-Columbian Art: the Roberts Wood Bliss Collection*.
  London: Phaidon.
McConnell, Kathleen, 1987, 'Plant dyeing in Peru'. *Journal for Weavers, Spinners and Dyers* 141: 16 and 18.
Means, Philip Ainsworth, 1930, *Peruvian Textiles: Examples of the Pre-Incaic Period*.
  New York: Metropolitan Museum of Art.
————, 1931, *Ancient Civilizations of the Andes*.
  New York and London: Charles Scribner's Sons.
————, 1932, *A Study of Peruvian Textiles*.
  Boston, Mass.: Museum of Fine Arts.
Meisch, Lynn A. (ed), 1997, *Traditional Textiles of the Andes*.
  London: Thames and Hudson.
Mullins, Barbara, 1974, 'Natural dyes of Peru'. *Quarterly Journal of the Guilds of Weavers, Spinners and Dyers* 89: 1825–7.
O'Neale, Lila M., 1942, 'Textile periods in ancient Peru: II, Paracas Caverns and the Grand Necropolis'. *American Archaeology and Ethnology* 39 (2): 143–202.
Poma de Ayala, Felipe Guaman, 1968, *Nuevo coronica y buen gobierno (Codex péruvien illustré)*.
  Paris: Institut d'Ethnologie.
Prescott, W. H., [1847, 1882] 1963, *The Conquest of Peru*.
  London: Everyman's Library.
Reid, James W., 1986, *Textile Masterpieces of Ancient Peru*.
  New York: Dover Publications.
Rowe, Ann Pollard, 1977, *Warp-Patterned Weaves of the Andes*.
  Washington DC: Textile Museum.
Rowe, John Howland, 1979, 'Standardization in Inca tapestry tunics'. In *Junius B. Bird Pre-Columbian Textile Conference*: 239–64.
  Washington DC: Textile Museum.
Sawyer, A. R., 1963, *Tiahuanaco Tapestry Design*. Studies 3.
  New York: Museum of Primitive Art.
Seagroatt, Margaret, 1984, 'The textile fibres: Part 3, Hairs'. *Journal for Weavers, Spinners and Dyers* 132: 18–20.
Tidball, Harriet, 1969, *Peru: Textiles Unlimited*. Monographs 25 and 26.
  Michigan: Shuttle Craft Guild.
VanStan, Ina, 1979, 'Did Inca weavers use an upright loom?'. In *Junius B. Bird Pre-Columbian Textile Conference*: 233–8.
  Washington DC: Textile Museum.
Vreeland, James M. Jr, 1986, 'Cotton spinning and processing on the Peruvian north coast', in *Junius B. Bird Conference on Andean Textiles*: 363–83.
  Washington DC: Textile Museum.
Wallace, Dwight T., 1979, 'The process of weaving development on the Peruvian coast', in *Junius B. Bird Pre-Colombian Textile Conference*: 27–50.
  Washington DC: Textile Museum.

ILLUSTRATION ACKNOWLEDGEMENTS

The information below is additional to that given in the captions

Page 2 Kate Olver
Page 6 Alison Mitchell
Fig.
1   Petrie Museum, University College London, U.C.9547
2   Klaus-Otto Hundt
3   British Museum Education Service
4   From Eva Wilson, *Ancient Egyptian Designs*, London, 1986
5   Peter Stalker, OXFAM
6   Ann Hecht
7   Susi Dunsmore
8   British Museum
9   Alison Mitchell
10   Gigi Crocker
11   Veronica Johnston
12   Gigi Crocker
13   VIDOC, Department of the Royal Tropical Institute, Amsterdam
14–17 Margaret Tebbs
18–19 Jenny Balfour-Paul
20–21 Ann Hecht
22–4 Margaret Tebbs
25   Photo Ann Hecht
26–8 Ann Hecht
29   British Museum 1974 Am.7.1. Photo Ann Hecht
30   British Museum 1971 Af.36.Q
31   British Museum 1900.36. Photo Ann Hecht
32–3 Ann Hecht
34   Victoria and Albert Museum I.S. 53-1966
35   Victoria and Albert Museum I.S. 55-1966
36   British Museum 1975 As.7.2. Photo Ann Hecht
37   Gigi Crocker
38   Ann Hecht
39   British Museum 1974 Am.7.1
40   Ann Hecht
41   American and Commonwealth Arts Section, University of Exeter
42   Reproduced by permission of the American Museum in Britain, Bath. 1880 90.78.31
43   Margaret Tebbs
44   A. L. Shuffrey FRPS
45   British Museum.
     (a) 1848 Am.17.28; (b) 1976 Am.5.1; (c) 1974 Am.3.102; (d) 1976 Am.3.100
46   British Museum 1976 Am.5.1. Photo Ann Hecht
47   British Museum 1948 Am.17.26. Photo Ann Hecht
48   British Museum 1976 Am.3.100. Photo Ann Hecht
49   Ann Hecht
50   British Museum 1974 Am.7.1. Photo Ann Hecht
51   Photo Ann Hecht
52–3 Gigi Crocker
54   Ann Hecht
55–6 Klaus-Otto Hundt
57   From Eva Wilson, *Ancient Egyptian Designs*, London 1986
58   British Museum 1975 As.3.1. Photo Ann Hecht
59–61 Ann Hecht
62   British Museum 1975 As.7.2. Photo Ann Hecht
63   British Museum 1975 As.3.3. Photo Ann Hecht
64   British Museum 1975 As.7.4. Photo Ann Hecht
65–6 British Museum 1975 As.7.2
66   Photo Ann Hecht
67–8 British Museum 1975 As.7.7. Photos Ann Hecht
69   Gigi Crocker
70–72 British Museum 1974 As.29.5
71–2 Photos Ann Hecht
73   British Museum 1966 Af.1.19
74–7 Nancy Stanfield
78   Photo Nancy Stanfield, copyright Horniman Museum
79   Nancy Stanfield
80   Photo Nancy Stanfield, copyright Horniman Museum
81–2 Nancy Stanfield
83   Museum für Völkerkunde, Basle, III 20236
84   British Museum 1971 Af.36.JP
85   British Museum 1934 3–7 127
86   British Museum 1980 Af.17.1
87–8 Ann Hecht
89   British Museum 1955 Af.5.252
90   Ann Hecht
91   Victoria and Albert Museum I.S.49-1966
92   Ann Hecht
93   British Museum 1905 362
94   Tony Tompson
95–6 VIDOC, Department of the Royal Tropical Institute, Amsterdam
97   Tony Tompson
98   Susi Dunsmore
99   Photo Ann Hecht
100 Victoria and Albert Museum I.S.49-1966
101 Victoria and Albert Museum I.S.53-1966
102 British Museum As.1980.A8
103 Ann Hecht
104 Victoria and Albert Museum I.S.55-1966. Photo Ann Hecht
105 Victoria and Albert Museum I.S.17-1960
106 Alison Mitchell
107 Victoria and Albert Museum T.329-1960
108–11 Alison Mitchell
112 Margaret Tebbs
113 Alison Mitchell
114 British Museum JA 1942-9-18-01
115 British Museum JA 1908-7-18-11
116 Alison Mitchell
117–19 Ann Hecht
120 Victoria and Albert Museum T.325-1960
121 Lawrence Cresswell
122 Ann Hecht
123 Susi Dunsmore
124 British Museum
125 Photo Susi Dunsmore, Crown copyright, Overseas Development Natural Resources Institute
126 British Museum
127–8 Susi Dunsmore
129 Mary Whorlow
130 Veronica Johnston
131–4 Susi Dunsmore
135 British Museum
136 Victoria and Albert Museum T.39-1931
137 Marianne Straub
138 British Museum 1977 Am.5.5
139 Marianne Straub
140 Ann Hecht
141 Margaret Tebbs
142 A. C. Gonzales, OXFAM
143 Marianne Straub
144 Margaret Sowden
145 British Museum 1983 Am.13.1. Photo Ann Hecht
146 Photo Ann Hecht
147 Ann Hecht
148 British Museum Am.1982.A16.7 Ann Hecht
149 Photo Ann Hecht
150 British Museum 1973 Am.3.114. Photo Ann Hecht
151 British Museum
152 Photo Jian Chen
153 Ann Hecht
154 British Museum XX.11/1
155 British Museum
156–7 From the chronicle of Guaman Poma de Ayala
158 British Museum 1913.10.21.1
159–60 British Museum
161–2 Ann Hecht
163 British Museum 1954 W.Am.5.477
164 Photo Rodrick Owen
165–6 Ann Hecht
167 British Museum 1913.3.11.1

INDEX

safflower (*Carthamus tinctorius*) 22, 67, 130
sage brush *50*
Salcaja (Guatemala) 160
Salt, Sir Titus 187
San Antonio Aguas Calientes (Guatemala)
   177
   textiles from *170, 178*
San Juan Sacatepeques (Guatemala) 163
sanyan 87
Sarawak 103, 109
Schmidt-Thome, M. 149
sericulture 17, 109, 123, 126–9, *127*
   see also *mawata*; silk
servilleta 158, 159, 160, 170
shed 13, *60*, 68, 69, 76, 105, 106, 132
   counter-, 13, *60, 61*, 68, 69, 76, 132
shed rod/roll 106, 132, 168, *169, 170*, 172
shed stick 13, *60, 62, 64*
sheep 17, 58, 61, 65, 87, 164
   baruwal *146, 148*
   Navaho 41
Sherpa 142, 146, 148, 152, 157
ship cloths *36, 101, 103, 116*
   see also *palepai; tampan*
Sierra Leone 87–9, 96
silk 16–18, 87, 109, 125–9, *127–9*, 165
   see also *mawata*; sericulture
silk cloth from Ryukyu Islands *6, 122*, 123
silk grass 109
silk moth (*Bombyx mori*) 17, 109, 126
   wild (*Anaphe panda*) 82, 87
   see also sericulture
songket 113
spindle 19
   ancient Egyptian 20
   bedouin 65, 67
   Guatemalan 164
   Navaho 19, 43, 46–8
   Nepalese 146
   Peruvian 184, *185*
   West African *88, 89*
spindle shaft 20, 46, 65
spindle whorl 19, 20, 48, 65, 184
spinner, hand held *165*
spinning 16, 18
   bedouin *18, 20*, 65–7
   drop and spin method of 19, 20, 65,
      89, 188
   Guatemalan *163, 164, 165*
   Indonesian 21, 107–9, *108*
   Nepalese 19, 146–8
   Peruvian 184–8, *188, 191*
   West African *83*, 87, 88
   see also drafting; plying
spinning wheel 20, *21*, 165
   rimless *21*, 107–8, *108*, 146
   treadle 23, 146
Stanley, Martha 79
stannous chloride, *see* mordants and
   auxiliaries, tin
Start, Laura E., *see* Haddon, Alfred C.
Stephens, John Lloyd 166
Strobilanthes flaccidifolius, see indigo
   dyeing plants

Sulawesi (Indonesia) 109, 121
sumac (*Rhus* sp.) 48, 67
Sumatra (Indonesia) 100, 103, 121
Sumba (Indonesia)
   hinggi shoulder cloth *102*
      weaving of *105*
   supplementary warp borders 37, 103,
      118, 119, 120
Sumbawa (Indonesia) 103
sword (beater) 15, 57, *60*–2, 76, 106, 134,
   168, 172, 177

tampan 36, 37, 103, *101*, 115, *116, 117*
tapestry 32, 52, 54–6, *56*, 57, 97, 173, *182,
   183*, 188, 192–6, *194*–7
tartan 106
   see also gingham
Tecpan (Guatemala), *huipil* from *179*
Tellem caves 73, 92
Tenganan Pegringsingan, Bali (Indonesia)
   106, *110*
tenter-hook 169
Thurstan, Violetta 64
Tiahuanica (Peru) 183, 193
Tomita, Jun and Norika 130
topi 142, 144, 155
Totonicapan (Guatemala) 162, 173
tsapola 149
tso (wild madder) 148
turmeric (*Curcuma* rhizome) 22, 111
tutze 159, 160
twining
   bedouin *38, 39, 66*, 68–70, *71*, 77, *78*
   Indonesian *120*, 121
   Navaho 44, *45, 54*
   Peruvian *180*

Upper Volta (West Africa) 82, 96

vicuna 17, 187

walnut (*Juglans* sp.) 23, 130, 150, 193
Warming, Wanda, and Michael Gaworski
   109, 112, 113
warp 9–14, 32, 43, 45, 46, 64, 97, 105,
   106, 121, 132–4, 137, 140, 153, 155,
   156, 160, 168–70, 172, 173, 183, 188,
   189, 192, 194–6
   discontinuous 183
   supplementary 37, *37*, 106, 118–20,
      118, 119, 121
warp beam 13, 106, 132, 134, 192
warp binding 134, *136*, 137; see also
   ikat; jaspe; kasuri
warp shifting box 137
warp spacer/spreader (raddle) 132, 137,
   173
warp threads 70, 194
warping 12, *12*, 44–6, 61–4, 74, 105, 155
warping board 12, *169, 170*
warping frame 44, *45*, 105
weave (textile structures)
   basket 35, 173
   bird's eye 35

brocading, *see separate entry*
finger-manipulated 144, *145*
ground 97, *100*, 115, *118*, 157
herringbone 35, 144
inlay *154*, 155–7, *155, 156*
plain (tabby), *see separate entry*
saha 69, *69*, 71, *71*–6
tapestry, *see separate entry*
twill 35, 97, 118, 144, *146, 146, 156*,
   177
twining, *see separate entry*
warp-faced 32, 59, 62, 64, 68, 77, 93,
   112, 121
wedge *56*
weft-faced *32*–4, 96, 112
   see also tapestry
weaving 32–9
   bedouin 68–79
   Guatemalan 173–9
   Indonesian 112–21
   Navaho 41–3, 52–7
   Nepalese 155–7
   Peruvian 193–6
   West African narrow strip 80–3, 93–9
weft 9, 13, 15, 32, 35, 38, 52–4, 61, 70,
   76, 93, 96, 106, 129, 134, 137, 140,
   160, 188, 193–6
   curvilinear *195, 196*
   ground 157
   supplementary 36, 37
      Guatemalan 173
      Indonesian 36, 37, 112–17, 103, 106
      Nepalese *154*, 155–7, *156*
      West African 97, *99*
weft binding 137–8
   see also *kasuri*
wefts, multiple 173
Weir, Shelagh 67
weld (*Reseda luteola*) 27, 30, *30*
woad (*Isatis tinctoria*) 26
wool 16, 17, 41, 43, 46, 48, 49, 59, 61,
   64, 65, 82, 87, 146, 164, 187, 188, 193
   see also alpaca; cashmere; guanaco;
   llama; vicuna

Yanagi, Yoshita 132
yarns
   acrylic 144, 164, 165
   bedouin 59, 65, 67, 68
   commercial 48
   Guatemalan 164, 165
   Navaho 43, 46–8
      Germantown 43, 47, 48
      Saxony 48
   Nepalese 146–8, 155, 156
   Peruvian 184, *185*, 188, 193, 194
   ravelled 43, 87, 88
   rayon 88, 165
   West African 87, *88*, 89, 93
yeibichai rugs 57, *57*
Yoruba, Nigeria *81, 86*, 93
Young, Stella 49
yucca 49, *50*